w/ Stephen Rhinesmith

⊗ Read "The Extreme Future" by James Canton
- INFO tech
- BIO Tech
- NANO Tech
- NEURO TECH

LEADERS NEED TO know:
- WHO THEY ARE
- WHAT are you trying to accomplish
- WHAT THEY WANT TO BE KNOWN FOR
AND WHAT courage will BE REQUIRED).

· BE A CONTEXT LEADER, NOT CONTENT LEADER
(CORRELATE AND STEER; INCLUDE THE "EXPERTS"
IN DETAILS)

" RELATIONSHIPS ARE THE KEY TO SUCCESS,
BUT ARE THE CHALLENGE IN GLOBAL ORGS".
[I think video-conf technology is key, but
not the basis for forming relationship —
RATHER for sustaining relationship].

BECOME "STAKEHOLDER-SAVVY".

PROBLEM vs. PARADOX:
- Problems HAVE a solution
∘ PARADOX HAVE TO BE KEPT IN BALANCE/OPTIMIZED
AS THERE IS NO PERMANENT solution.

P9-CFD-359

LEADING IN TIMES OF CRISIS

With best wishes

LEADING IN TIMES OF CRISIS

Navigating Through Complexity, Diversity, and Uncertainty to Save Your Business

DAVID L. DOTLICH
PETER C. CAIRO
STEPHEN H. RHINESMITH

DELTA ORGANIZATION & LEADERSHIP LLC

JOSSEY-BASS
A Wiley Imprint
www.josseybass.com

Copyright © 2009, Delta Organization & Leadership LLC.

Published by Jossey-Bass
A Wiley Imprint
989 Market Street, San Francisco, CA 94103-1741—www.josseybass.com

No part of this publication may be reproduced, stored in a retrieval system, or transmitted in any form or by any means, electronic, mechanical, photocopying, recording, scanning, or otherwise, except as permitted under Section 107 or 108 of the 1976 United States Copyright Act, without either the prior written permission of the publisher, or authorization through payment of the appropriate per-copy fee to the Copyright Clearance Center, Inc., 222 Rosewood Drive, Danvers, MA 01923, 978-750-8400, fax 978-646-8600, or on the Web at www.copyright.com. Requests to the publisher for permission should be addressed to the Permissions Department, John Wiley & Sons, Inc., 111 River Street, Hoboken, NJ 07030, 201-748-6011, fax 201-748-6008, or online at www.wiley.com/go/permissions.

Readers should be aware that Internet Web sites offered as citations and/or sources for further information may have changed or disappeared between the time this was written and when it is read.

Limit of Liability/Disclaimer of Warranty: While the publisher and author have used their best efforts in preparing this book, they make no representations or warranties with respect to the accuracy or completeness of the contents of this book and specifically disclaim any implied warranties of merchantability or fitness for a particular purpose. No warranty may be created or extended by sales representatives or written sales materials. The advice and strategies contained herein may not be suitable for your situation. You should consult with a professional where appropriate. Neither the publisher nor author shall be liable for any loss of profit or any other commercial damages, including but not limited to special, incidental, consequential, or other damages.

Jossey-Bass books and products are available through most bookstores. To contact Jossey-Bass directly call our Customer Care Department within the U.S. at 800-956-7739, outside the U.S. at 317-572-3986, or fax 317-572-4002.

Jossey-Bass also publishes its books in a variety of electronic formats. Some content that appears in print may not be available in electronic books.

Library of Congress Cataloging-in-Publication Data

Dotlich, David L. (David Landreth).
    Leading in times of crisis : navigating through complexity, diversity, and uncertainty to save your business / David L. Dotlich, Peter C. Cairo, Stephen H. Rhinesmith.—1st ed.
        p. cm.
    Includes bibliographical references and index.
    ISBN 978-0-470-40230-6 (cloth)
        1. Leadership.   2. Management.   3. Success in business.   I. Cairo, Peter C.
II. Rhinesmith, Stephen H.   III. Title.
HD57.7.D676 2009
658.4'056—dc22
                                                                            2009001146

Printed in the United States of America
FIRST EDITION
HB Printing   10 9 8 7 6 5 4 3 2 1

Contents

LEADING IN TIMES OF CRISIS

Introduction

WHEN WE MET WITH THE CEO OF A MAJOR corporation recently, we asked him how things were going. Rather than giving us a typical response—"fine" or "good, except for problem x"—he responded with a sigh. He began talking about how his job never stops; how he's under incredible stress; how there's too much information to digest and too many decisions to make; how he feels as if the credit crisis, stock market fluctuations, and global economy are weighing him down; how it's impossible to know the right thing to do. Obviously, we had caught him on a bad day.

We should add that this is a prominent CEO with outstanding business results, a global brand with huge equity, and a top-tier team around him. His complaints were revealing that day, but given his success we could only imagine how other leaders, less successful and well resourced, must feel.

Actually, we don't have to imagine it. In our work with top executive teams and interviews with global executives, we've talked to leaders in a variety of industries about their perspectives on the complexities, diversity issues, and uncertain situations they face. What we've found is that the contradictions, challenges, and opportunities of the leadership role continue to multiply each year. Each day seems to bring new complications, and the conflicting needs of investors, customers, employees, and regulators increase with globalization, technology, and regulation. Many leaders worry that the global meltdown in credit and the worldwide need for governments to shore up the banking

1

system have created new levels of complexity and uncertainty for leaders at all levels and in all industries.

Leaders tell us that in a world of unpredictable and uncharted events they worry about what's going to happen next. They worry that when they walk into the office or go online, watch CNN, or answer their cell phone, a surprise will be waiting that would force them to rethink their entire business. It might be global financial uncertainty, lack of alignment in a matrixed organization, limited viability of a current business or profit model, or the increasing expectations (and options) of major customers. And the quarterly, monthly, even weekly demand to deliver better results does not stop. As a leader, you can probably relate to these challenges. Uncertainty is going to be with us for a while.

As stressful as your current business environment is, it probably also contains an almost sinful abundance of opportunities. New technologies enable convergence and connection, and rapidly emerging global markets and innovative, breakthrough services and solutions all create strategic growth opportunities that never existed before. Taking advantage of them in a volatile, unpredictable world, of course, requires leaders who can make savvy decisions and move quickly even as the earth shifts beneath their feet. The constraints imposed by credit restrictions may also hold competitors back. The new shape of financial services, banking, and government involvement in lending is putting new emphasis on efficiency, return on assets, and cash flow. Smart leaders will get ready for this—and will thrive as a result.

Unfortunately, some leaders are more likely to become unbalanced by these seismic shifts than to think clearly, feel deeply, and act decisively. This is understandable, since a good percentage of today's leaders have been selected, developed, and rewarded for a more stable time. In most companies, intelligence, fitting in, perseverance, and results—however short term—have been the ticket to the top. These are admirable qualities—but they are no longer enough. We have found that successful CEOs are using a range of leadership skills that constitute an almost holistic leadership style, one not easily described by most corporate competency models.

In the past, gradual experience—gained over time in a variety of situations—was the best predictor of success in a senior corporate role.

Companies defined and replicated effective leadership by investing heavily in competency-based leadership development, parsing leadership behaviors and skills, assessing leaders against those behaviors, and prescribing experiences and assignments to produce those behaviors. But today a lot of incremental, similar experience from the past may not be relevant in addressing current challenges; skills gained in a more stable environment may not produce the judgment necessary in the newly complex, diverse, and uncertain business context.

Many CEOs have told us that if they had listened to their gut, they might have satisfied themselves with lower returns, even if their job was on the line for insufficient growth. Two years ago we published a book based on extensive research titled *Head, Heart, and Guts.* The thesis of the book, as the title suggests, is that effective leaders are *whole leaders,* leaders who use their head to set strategy, their heart to connect with the world, and their guts to make instinctive and intuitive decisions based on clear values. Since then, and despite the book's wide acceptance as a leadership model by a number of large global companies, we still too often see top business executives attempting to solve problems or seize opportunities using only their head . . . or their heart . . . or their guts.

We've learned that no matter how smart you are, you can't out-think every problem. Likewise, no matter how empathic you are, people skills will be ineffective when you try to deal with complex trade-offs, and no matter how quick you are to roll the dice and take action, getting things done may not grow or move the business if you're doing the wrong things. Given the increasing demands on organizations and those who lead them, becoming a whole leader will become as important as experience in determining leadership success in the future. Using your head to anticipate, understand, analyze, and respond to new strategic directions, your heart to see the world from the perspective of a diverse range of stakeholders, and your guts to make tough decisions based on clear values will be the key leadership navigation tools that you will have as you make your way through the storms of uncertainty, diversity, and complexity that will constitute the environment for all leaders in the future.

We've written this book as an extension of our earlier work. We believe that there continues to be a shortage of talented leaders in most organizations. Most companies continue to rely on, promote, and reward one-dimensional leadership. Leaders and companies are unprepared for the increasing technological, environmental, and global demands on leadership that, combined with increased regulations and decreased credit, will require radical rethinking of what constitutes effective leadership and how to produce it. Our hope is that this book will give you the insights and tools to prepare yourself and others to succeed in the complex and uncertain business world we all face.

PART
ONE

The Challenge

Navigating the Perfect Storm

Complexity, Diversity, and Uncertainty

I T STARTED LIKE ALL STORMS—THE BREEZE BEGAN TO PICK UP, but people didn't notice it right away. Then as technology made home computers and more efficient work systems a reality, people sensed that something was in the air. Everyone began talking about how these new inventions would reduce costs and allow people to enjoy life more with less effort.

As technology's impact grew stronger, it generated waves of new information, access to new markets, and the ability to incorporate diverse views and interests when making decisions. People grew excited about these changes because things seemed to be coming together—integrated solutions, integrated organizations, global perspectives combined with local needs—all addressed simultaneously in increasing detail through integrated technology.

But sometime around the turn of the twenty-first century, the speed of technology joined with the increased diversity of perspectives and possibilities, and the climate became highly uncertain. Old assumptions about business began to be swept away, new voices entered the discussion, and leaders began to feel challenged and worried.

Suddenly, even the most accomplished leaders became uncertain about how to lead in this volatile, unpredictable environment.

The metaphor of a perfect storm captures the current environment perfectly. We are witnessing the rare convergence of complexity and diversity, a convergence that challenges all our leadership assumptions. Imagine leaders as captains steering ships through this perfect storm. The old charts are outdated, and even the smartest strategists have not yet been able to adequately map a new world. Every time someone conducts a study of the new territory, the storm starts shoaling the terrain and changing the navigation lanes. As fast as leaders develop new strategies, powerful external forces render them obsolete.

In such times, leaders need to rely on their own beliefs and instincts, and on those of their people. During a perfect storm, things move too fast amid too much chaos to permit long periods of study and deliberation. Like the best captains trying to keep their ships afloat during the fiercest storms, leaders have to depend on what they know to be true. They also have to depend on the advice and suggestions of others. Judgment can be skewed when things get rough and it's impossible to see any blue sky ahead. In these difficult moments, leaders must lean on a range of advisers and then make their decisions. This is true not just for a day or two, but for weeks, months, and even years, since the storm shows no sign of abating. Even though goals may change and directions shift, leaders must keep moving.

These are not times for average leaders or for those who cannot appreciate and use the skills of all their key people. If this perfect storm is to be navigated, it will take whole leaders who use their full potential to move the enterprise through an enormously complex, diverse, and uncertain era.

Translating Metaphor into Meta-Challenges

Leaders now confront huge challenges that must somehow be understood and acted upon. As formidable as these challenges might be during normal times, during a perfect storm they appear insurmountable. They're not, but that's not to deny how confusing they are when you can't get your bearings. Consider these very real scenarios, which senior executives we know have recently faced:

- You would like to charter a new team to look at business prospects in an emerging market. None of your direct reports have lived or worked extensively outside your home country, but your growth projections for emerging markets next year are expected to triple.

- You have been asked by colleagues in another sector of your company to work together to develop a global franchise of products that will cut across country business units. You wonder if getting involved in such an intangible project is wise, given the daunting numbers you must achieve by year-end and the amount of effort that will be required to get country managers on board.

- Your top team of analysts is proposing a business idea to sell a new type of financing to accompany your major product line. The underlying debt will be repackaged and sold to various investors and financial institutions. You're familiar with business finance but don't fully understand the debt structure and degree of risk. However, you have watched your competitors make huge profits by offering financing to their customers and you have confidence in the "quants" proposing this product. Do you follow the herd and, if so, how much of your own balance sheet are you willing to commit? What is your appetite for risk?

- You are preparing next year's business plan, and your strategic planning group is unable to predict with any degree of precision the price of commodities for the next twelve months.

- You want to visit some key customers who have called to complain about the lack of innovation in your product offerings. You open your electronic calendar and realize that every hour of every day is scheduled for the next three months.

- You work in a regulated industry and are leading a task force reviewing clinical trials of a future product offering. The clinical results are ambiguous. Sponsoring additional trials will cost millions of dollars and cause months if not years of delay before introducing the new product, which may generate millions in new revenue. However, product liability could also create years of litigation.

These are simple, even simplistic, examples of the types of challenges leaders face every day in dealing with complexity, diversity, and uncertainty. But they are real and capture the dilemmas of leading in modern companies. The perfect storm is here. The extent to which leaders are able to meet these new challenges will determine whether they (and their companies) survive, much less succeed.

A VIEW FROM THE BRIDGE: WATCHING COMPLEXITY, DIVERSITY, AND UNCERTAINTY IN ACTION

We have served as business advisers to CEOs and boards on issues of talent and leadership for many years in many companies and in many countries. We have built one of the premier firms for educating senior executives outside business schools; every week, around the world, we work closely with CEOs, executive teams, and individual leaders. We have had the privilege of working with some of the best leaders in some of the best companies, including Nike, Johnson & Johnson, Avon, Colgate-Palmolive, Fidelity, Doosan, Merck, Novartis, and many others. We routinely hear that the intersection of technology, media, regulatory bodies, shareholder activism, politics, people, and competition has created a dynamic playing field with almost unfathomable risk and uncertain opportunity. Everywhere leaders are saying the same thing: The complexity, diversity, and uncertainty of their world have increased, and their leadership ability is not keeping pace.

The *complexity* of issues faced by leaders at each level of every company today is significant. More information, more opinions, more connectedness, and more options have made understanding what is going on difficult; it is even more difficult to make decisions, often quickly, about matters that you don't understand. Organizations now comprise multiple reporting relationships, often in far-flung geographies, that all require numerous inputs before decisions can be made. New information appears daily—even hourly—over the Internet. Customers, competitors, and partners often overlap, and loyalties are often unclear.

As a result, many leaders feel trapped and sometimes overwhelmed by complexity. They try to figure it out by increasing the amount of information they digest each day, or holding more meetings, or reading and responding to all the e-mail they receive. They search for decision tools, time-saving approaches, and new ways to organize themselves. They recognize the leader's job is to sort through complexity, but are unclear how to read the ever-changing environment.

Complexity multiplies upon itself. Organizations, information, markets, globalization, and people all come together to confuse and confound many leaders today. More than one leader has told us, "I try to focus on the high-priority, high-payoff activities." But this usually means sacrificing the long term in favor of the short term—in effect, giving up efforts to find a map through the storm and concentrating on getting to the nearest shore.

For leaders, the world has become flatter, faster, more interdependent, and riskier. Regulatory decisions in one country now spread worldwide. The outcomes of clinical trials in China now influence regulatory approvals in the United States. Consumer reactions to product introductions are now instantly global. Financial decisions made in one country by one company—and even one leader—can shake the global financial system. Large corporations such as Bear Stearns, Countrywide, Lehman Brothers, Merrill Lynch, Arthur Andersen, and (as everyone knows) Enron, can disappear overnight as a result of a few wrong decisions. Brands that have enjoyed trust and allegiance for decades can be eroded instantly by the actions of a few people. In the face of increasing complexity, is it any wonder leaders tread more carefully as they assess their choices?

But what feels like a trap is really a paradox, and there is an important difference. For example, no one disputes the importance of knowledge—but too much knowledge can be a bad thing. Most leaders look for the "sweet spot" between making problems overly complex by analyzing them to death and overly simple by ignoring critical facts that can tilt a decision in one direction or another. We'll talk a lot about understanding paradox as a tool for managing complexity, because facing a range of conflicting choices is often what drives the perception of complexity.

No one will argue that the diversity of people—diverse in terms of their backgrounds, values, and cultures—has increased exponentially and also presents a challenging piece of the new leadership environment. Because of globalization, immigration, and, yes, technology, diversity has become a priority for every company and leadership team. Leaders who fail to acknowledge and capitalize on the increasing differences among their employees, customers, and markets run the risk of losing touch with these key stakeholders.

Changing consumer tastes, widening generation gaps, and intensifying cultural differences, accompanied by proliferating product and service choices, create daunting diversity and complexity.

Most leaders have never had to operate in such a complexly diverse and diversely complex environment. Just consider one issue to glimpse the magnitude of the problems (and opportunities) for leaders. Immediate access to information through multiple channels has put the power of choice in the hands of consumers, customers, clients, and patients, placing extraordinary pressure on leaders to truly understand their needs at a deep level. Companies such as Nike, Kraft, Harley-Davidson, and Colgate are all focusing on developing markets as an important source of growth. However, simply exporting U.S. products and marketing to developing countries does not do the job. Leaders in these companies are working hard to see the world through the eyes of their diverse new consumers. We take senior leaders in our action learning programs to India, China, Vietnam, and Brazil and immerse them in the lives of their future customers—sitting on the beds in one-room huts to understand the daily routines and grasp the hopes and dreams of the people they hope to serve. Diversity today is mastering the art of walking a mile in someone else's shoes—someone with whom you have little in common—so you can adapt to their expectations and appreciate their strengths—or else prepare to be overtaken by competitors in emerging markets who will soon be expanding into the developed world. Diversity is both an urgent challenge and an urgent opportunity.

Leaders tell us constantly about the challenge of taking action in the face of *uncertainty*. Or, more specifically, they complain about the difficulty of doing so. The world is becoming a less predictable place, but the demand for action in the face of uncertainty is unrelenting. One executive recently said that in his job, complexity creates uncertainty. While the overall amount of information is increasing, he must make highly complex decisions based on less information than he's used to having. Because the speed of change has increased exponentially, he lacks the time to agonize about what he doesn't know. As he put it: "All you can ask is whether you're missing something that is available." At that point you have to rely on your personal beliefs, values, and sense of purpose to move forward. Otherwise, you will be left standing on the sidelines while your customers, competitors, stakeholders, and employees move on.

One aspect of uncertainty for all leaders, whether they realize it or not, is the intersection of climate change, oil prices, environmental concern, and alternative energy, which may impact every business model of every company throughout the world. In *Flat, Hot and Crowded,* Thomas Friedman points out that destabilizing climate change and competition for energy will soon affect everyone—especially companies seeking energy, transporting products, and producing waste—and will forever change how business is conducted. Friedman also points out, however, that the opportunities created by the demand for alternative energy will be as significant as those of the information revolution.

The other aspect of uncertainty for leaders today is the global financial and credit system, which has absorbed significant shocks recently, consolidated in the aftermath of many bank failures, and faces a period of regulation, conservative decision making, and credit tightening likely to last for years. The global credit crisis, which began with sub-prime lending in the United States, has demonstrated that the financial system, including derivatives, hedge funds, collateralized debt, currency trading, and energy speculation is now fully global, not very transparent, and extends around the world. The business plan of a leader in Iowa to acquire a competitor in Denmark is subject to disruption by the lending practices of a bank in New York with a creditor in Thailand. Of course, no leader can be expected to track all this interdependency, but the resulting complexity is a structural factor that creates insecurity and more uncertainty today than ever before.

The Whole Leadership Imperative

We work with many global companies to prepare their leaders for the future. The first step is to define what successful leaders will look like. Here's what one of our Fortune 100 clients expects its successful executives to be able to do:

- Find continued sources of innovation and growth with an emphasis on emerging markets.
- Navigate through a set of complex external legal challenges, regulatory hurdles, media onslaughts, and policy threats.

- Demonstrate resiliency in the face of uncertain challenges.
- Be accepted by employees as a reputable steward of the firm.
- Represent the company externally and be its credible public face to multiple stakeholders.
- Display the will and physical energy to do the job.

It's a long list, but this description is not unique given the future environment most companies anticipate, and it acknowledges that complexity, diversity, and uncertainty will be the ongoing context for leading. Given the increasing demands on organizations and those who lead them, becoming a "whole leader" will be critical to navigating this perfect storm.

We've watched successful leaders manage this new environment, from companies as diverse as BP, Nike, Novartis, Doosan, Fidelity, and many others. Many of their stories are contained in the following pages. One lesson emerges as a starting point: *you can't break down complexity, diversity, and uncertainty into piece parts and manage each separately.* Too often, we see top business executives attempting to solve problems or seize opportunities using only their head . . . or heart . . . or guts. We've learned that no matter how smart you are, you can't outthink every problem; that no matter how empathic you are, your people skills will be ineffective in certain situations; that no matter how quick you are to roll the dice and take action, getting the wrong things done will not help the business.

As a leader you must bring it all together by bringing yourself together. You must use your head to anticipate, understand, analyze, and respond to new strategic directions, your heart to see the world from the perspective of a diverse range of stakeholders, and your guts to make tough decisions based on clear values. This is a simple description of "whole leadership," and one companies such as Bank of America, Kraft, KPMG, Colgate, Merck, and many others are adopting because it captures in simple terms the complicated components of leading today.

Keep our metaphor in mind: A perfect storm requires leaders to possess a wide range of navigation tools. You can't lead as you have in the past. You must tap into the capacities of your head, heart, and guts as increasingly volatile and unpredictable situations dictate.

We've written this book because we see a shortage of talented leaders in most organizations to deal with the perfect storm, and we see so many companies continuing to rely on, promote, and reward one-dimensional leadership. Leaders and companies are unprepared for the spiraling technological, environmental, and global demands on leadership, which require radical rethinking of what constitutes effective leadership and how to produce it.

In the next chapter, we present what we mean by complexity, diversity, and uncertainty. Subsequent chapters describe the how-to when it comes to navigating the storm. At the end, we provide ways you can develop yourself, build your team, and lead your company through the tumult and confusion ahead.

The challenges that leaders face today have no easy answers, and what works for one leader may not directly apply to another. But we hope this book will give you some ideas, insights, and even tools that will help you survive and thrive in uniquely challenging times.

What You're Up Against as a Leader Today

HAVEN'T THINGS ALWAYS BEEN COMPLEX, DIVERSE, AND uncertain? For at least the past thirty years or so, haven't leaders struggled with information overload, issues involving minorities, and a volatile marketplace?

Yes, to a certain degree. But not to the degree of today's perfect storm. It is absolutely impossible to overestimate the turbulence and chaos that leaders now confront every day. If leaders are honest, they'll admit that they don't always know what to do; that they're constantly facing right-versus-right choices; that they are leading a growing number of people with whom they have little in common; that their businesses and industries are so unpredictable that even if everything seems to be going great, it can all go to hell in a handbasket overnight. Remember the three leaders of the auto industry trying to explain how and why they needed a government bailout for a market that had crashed in a matter of months?

This perfect storm of complexity, diversity, and uncertainty is here to stay, at least for the foreseeable future. It therefore behooves every leader to understand its elements and how they have come together to create such a challenging and confusing climate. To that end, this chapter digs deeper into each of these elements, starting with complexity.

Viewing Complexity Through a Distorted Lens

Leaders long for clarity, and in most cases, they're not going to get it. This isn't just because they have too much information to process—the standard definition of complexity. Rather, it's because various other elements distort the view of complex matters.

Take the case of the recent home mortgage crisis: Very smart, very experienced CEOs, including Chuck Prince, Peter Wuffli, Kerry Killinger, and Stan O'Neal, lost their jobs because their skill and experience did not serve them in navigating the forced choice of lower returns or higher, almost unfathomable risk. Sub-prime financial modeling has devastated more than one prominent financial services firm and killed others such as Bear Stearns and Lehman Brothers, and it's not because firm leaders were stupid.

Many industries have become highly specialized, and the greater the degree of specialization, the more complex things get. Very smart product developers lower down in the organization create new approaches that rely on such complex technical knowledge that senior leaders cannot possibly make judgments about the efficacy of the final product. In the banking system, problems developed because lenders didn't understand the risk portfolio of sub-prime loans, and many people at all levels lost their jobs because of these complexities.

It's also tough to focus on complex matters when anxiety and fear distort your view. Because of these challenging times, anxiety and fear are rampant. The answers to most problems are not obvious. When leaders try to deal with enormously complicated problems such as how much to centralize their business operations, what long-term investment is required for innovation, how to meet the regulatory requirements of Sarbanes-Oxley or increase minority representation in senior management, they face the uncertainty of choosing between two right causes. This, in turn, makes people anxious. Resources and time are limited, opportunities come and go quickly, and small problems can spiral into big ones. We have seen executives for whom this anxiety turns into outright fear when a crisis like a downsizing, acquisition, or lawsuit occurs. In such a fearful atmosphere, employees also resist change, making it difficult to implement anything new. We have worked with many CEOs and senior leaders to align their culture with a new business strategy only to have its implementation undermined not by rational analysis but by subtle and unspoken fear about change and the future.

Leaders themselves complain they can't figure things out, and often it's because their own fear and resistance cloud their vision. Leaders can't see patterns that would help them determine what to do because the atmosphere is thick with anxiety. But what is it that people want from their leaders during times like these? You don't have to look further than Yahoo chat boards and internal employee surveys for the answer:

- Where are we going and how will we get there?
- Are we going to be all right?
- What should my priorities be when there are so many demands?
- What do our leaders truly think and can I trust them?

We have also noticed this same confusion in senior management team meetings. We've witnessed back-and-forth debates about questions without clear answers as senior leaders argue for different outcomes, some of which are contradictory. One CEO we work with says that one by-product of this ambiguity is greater stress and conflict on management teams. The lack of clear answers to important questions leads to heated debates. A common example we have seen recently in U.S. or European companies is the debate about doing business in China. On one hand, people see enormous advantages in the opportunities China presents as a partner, supplier, and customer. On the other hand, Chinese companies also represent a huge threat to their business. Knowing how to handle these uncertainties is critical. The ability of a team to sort through alternatives and achieve alignment in the face of uncertainty can be a hallmark of its success.

The environment becomes even more complex when you add "new business models" into the mix. More and more organizations are shape-shifting to fit emerging realities, so it's tough to know how to restructure, let alone when and why. When leaders see a company like Lenovo emerge on the world scene, it has to make them stop and think . . . and wonder if they are hopelessly behind the times. Lenovo is a self-described "new world company," designed to blend best practices of both West and East. Originally a company called Legend founded by eleven Chinese computer scientists, it acquired IBM's

PC business in 2004; it now has operations all over the world and is targeting emerging markets such as Brazil and India. Lenovo doesn't fit any previous model, and its existence forces leaders to question their own models. In *Globality: Competing with Everyone from Everywhere for Everything,* three Boston Consulting Group consultants have documented some of the new ways of thinking that market leaders in emerging economies are using to enter the global marketplace. With a fierce emphasis on costs, education, local market knowledge, innovation, and thinking big while acting fast, these companies are turning many old Western assumptions and business models on their heads.

Complexity would be easier to deal with if Western leaders used more than their brains to grapple with it. Unfortunately, many extremely bright executives fall into the trap of trying to outthink complexity, and all they get for their efforts is a giant headache. Yes, leaders should use their head to understand evolving complex industry trends. But they should also rely on their heart to put themselves in the shoes of different customers and competitors. And they should have the guts to question conventional thinking and assumptions about their own business model and the future.

Whole leaders handle complexity well because they use a framework or filter to sort through existing data and are not paralyzed by having less information than they need or want. They possess a theory of the case, a way of viewing the world, and this allows them to strip away a lot of distracting and confusing elements of complex matters. They can focus in a way other leaders cannot. They can also take action in the midst of paralyzing complexity. And they can forge the trust that keeps a team together and moving forward during confusing times.

Johnson & Johnson is a company that is experiencing as much complexity as any other large global pharmaceutical and device manufacturer—regulatory requirements, fast-changing technologies, pricing pressures, growth in developing markets, and almost ongoing litigation. What does the chairman and CEO, Bill Weldon, do in response? He gathers his top hundred leaders together for an intense three-day discussion—to review, debate, and align around their corporate credo. He knows he can't teach his senior leaders everything they will need to know to manage the new complexities. But he believes that building and keeping trust with key constituencies will be critical for the future. His view is that leaders who combine head, heart, and guts in a shared understanding of and commitment to the J&J Credo will do better in managing the new complexities than leaders who are rigorously trained in the latest analytical tools and business acumen. Johnson & Johnson has navigated some of the recent perils of the pharmaceutical industry better than most.

Colgate-Palmolive is one of the most successful consumer products companies in the world. Under the leadership of former CEO Reuben Mark, the company established a nearly unparalleled track record of growth over the past two decades. While new CEO, Ian Cook, has continued the same, proven core business strategies, he recognizes that the challenges of leading today require additional capabilities. He is challenging Colgate leaders to find the right blend of skills between the old model that served the company so well and new competencies that will be required in the face of new challenges. He knows that the company must maintain its financial strength, ability to execute, and the strong values that have made it successful while becoming faster, more innovative, and even better at translating consumer needs into new products. He does not underestimate the complexity of the issues he faces in meeting these challenges. At the same time he knows that responding to them will require a combination of well-informed beliefs, business discipline, constant communication, and a culture that relies on people to do the right thing.

DIVERSITY AS A STRATEGIC IMPERATIVE

It is ironic that as the world of work becomes increasingly diverse, many leaders still grimace when you mention the word *diversity.* To them, the word connotes uncomfortable initiatives, political correctness, and forced rules. However, the importance of diversity is not going to diminish. But it must be redefined beyond traditional focus on internal diversity and seen as a strategic imperative that requires

- Understanding other cultures, stakeholders, and consumers
- Demonstrating real empathy and understanding of community concerns for sustainability and economic development

- Taking risks to do things differently by building the strategic alliances, coalitions, and relationships necessary to manage effectively in a complex world

Nike is a company with prospects for enormous future growth in China. Millions of Chinese consumers are learning the fun of sport, the pride of winning, and the power behind the Nike swoosh on shoes and apparel. China is one of Nike's biggest growth engines. To prepare for this explosive growth, we've helped Nike conduct many leadership programs in China during which their senior leaders spend time with young consumers, study a variety of retail formats, and interact with Chinese athletes. Nike's Chinese employees spend time with their counterparts in the United States, and Nike's board of directors has met in China. Diversity and inclusion mean different things in different countries and to different people. At Nike, diversity and inclusion are what drive creativity and innovation around growth, especially in a growth market like China.

We are in the midst of a diversity revolution. The topic has been around for years, but has recently taken on greatly expanded and altered meaning. When diversity first became an issue in organizations, it was primarily defined in racial terms. Then it broadened to encompass gender, ethnicity, and age. Nevertheless, it was still basically viewed by many companies as a compliance issue, a response to pressures from external constituencies or institutions like the federal government.

Recently, however, the topic has moved to a higher and more meaningful level—diversity has become the right thing to do for right-thinking organizations. Many factors have driven this evolution, especially the increasingly global way in which companies conduct business and the need to partner with people from a wide variety of countries.

During this evolution, all sorts of diversity training programs were created and everyone within an organization became aware of the need to create diverse teams and other integrated groups. However, the implementation of conventional diversity programs proved to have little impact. Seen as obligatory by many people, enrollment was often mandatory and participation was met with grudging acceptance. These programs were a defensive response to social inequities. More than that, diversity often became highly politicized, with people divided into the haves and have-nots. Contention was at the heart of diversity discussions, not collaboration. The adversarial aspect of many diversity programs created discomfort, even among those who were supportive. Furthermore, in a recent study of eight hundred companies reported by Kalev and others in the *Journal of Sociology,* those that had implemented standard diversity programs were actually found to be *less* diverse than they were before!

But now we've moved to the next phase in the evolution, one in which diversity has become a strategic imperative. Even the way in which diversity is taught has changed. Mahzarin Banaji, a professor at Harvard University, has conducted research about unconscious biases that affect all human beings regardless of their race, gender, ethnicity, or anything else in their background. She refers to these biases as "mind bugs" that affect the way people view others and the world around them. Rather than focusing only on traditional racial, ethnic, and gender bias, she argues that we all have subjective views that influence hiring and promotion decisions, who we listen to on our teams, what we believe about our customers, and how we collaborate both inside and outside our organizations. Furthermore, unless leaders understand their own unconscious biases, they are likely to inadvertently put constraints on their ability to bring maximum value to their companies. Her work provides a research-based and nonthreatening way for leaders to examine how they can build on diversity to create environments that are more inclusive for their people, customers, and clients.

Today, diversity means influencing key stakeholders. This is a huge evolutionary leap that might, in fact, be termed revolutionary—because the mind-set and attitude associated with this controversial term have changed that dramatically. Diversity used to be seen as a constraint; now it is seen as an asset. The ability to identify with another person's perspective—a perspective that differs significantly from your own—is how relationships are built and collaboration is enhanced. We're seeing this shift in the way politicians campaign, companies connect with their customers, and messages are conveyed to employees. Leaders need to empathize with constituencies that influence them or that they have influence on. This means customers, employees, competitors, suppliers, regulators, foreign market representatives, and foreign governments.

Yet we still see too many executives relying exclusively on building their own business case and talking about it with passion—or using the authority of their office to get things done within their organization.

This is fine in certain situations, but diversity demands other types of influence. Leaders frequently fail to ask questions to determine what the world looks like from other people's points of view. They may be eloquent and persuasive in stating their case, but unless they can empathize with others, and bring those perspectives into the organization, they will likely fail to be successful.

When people are not empathic, they lack one of the most important elements of leadership today—the ability to build trust, especially with those who are different from themselves. True empathy means having other people believe that you can place yourself in their shoes and feel what they feel—and use those feelings to develop responsive policies and practices. Organizational leaders can't impose their beliefs and structures on others and expect trust to flourish.

We should point out that despite the increased prominence of diversity issues in the business world, leadership ranks have not become correspondingly diverse, at least in many Western-based companies. In a January 2007 *Economist Intelligence Unit* article, Ashis Bhattacharya, global marketing director at Moog Industrial, asks, "Everyone views China and India as the emerging markets that will deliver the greatest business opportunity in coming years. But how many Fortune 500 board members are from either of these two markets?" The answer, of course, is very few.

Just as complexity sounds like a head issue, diversity topics like appreciating and integrating others from different cultures sound like heart issues. Again, though, the other two elements of whole leadership are crucial. You're not going to have true strategic diversity unless you can understand the needs of various stakeholder groups. And you're not going to achieve meaningful diversity unless you have the guts to implement programs that have a real impact (as opposed to traditional diversity training). We examine the mix of head, heart, and guts in dealing with complexity, diversity, and uncertainty in more detail in the next section of this book.

UNCERTAINTY: ACTING WHEN NOTHING CAN BE FULLY KNOWN

Every day, complexity and diversity seem to bring more uncertainty and paradox into our work lives. Risks—financial, strategic, brand,

and project risks—are multiplying. No leader or company can get enough information before making a truly good decision; in the short time between making a choice and implementing it, new data points are born that may render the choice flawed. Competitors emerge out of nowhere (especially in developing markets and sometimes with only incremental improvements on your own product). Technology innovation renders a huge capital investment obsolete. A customer acquisition model—for instance, a large sales force, that has served a company well for years—becomes an anachronism seemingly over-night as people move to the Internet for information and increased purchasing power.

Consider uncertainty within the context of growth. For many years, major corporations could grow with some predictability by process improvements, reinvestment of cost efficiencies, and acqui-sitions that yielded predictable returns. Attempts to grow through these and other traditional means no longer work—or at least not as well as before. The number one question on the mind of almost any CEO today is, Where is growth going to come from, and how is it going to be sustained? Having an answer to this question will mean the difference between short and long tenure for almost any CEO.

Perhaps the biggest challenge of uncertainty is the scarcity of definitive answers. It is difficult to know if a strategy will be effec-tive, even if it has been effective in the past. It is unclear if a younger generation of employees will be motivated by the same things that motivated an older generation. No matter how much research or how many resources are available, a leader still can't move forward with complete confidence. It's entirely possible that in a fast-moving world, something will take place in the next day or the next minute that will render that research obsolete or make those resources insufficient.

Consider NBC, which acquired the rights to the 2008 Olympics in Beijing. Its leaders decided to delay transmission of the opening ceremo-nies to prime time in the United States, only to find that viewers were searching global Internet sites to see the event live. When NBC won the rights to the Olympics years before the event, it thought it could count on a huge captive market for its programming. As it turned out, YouTube and others were able to show video of the events in Beijing almost immediately, giving viewers an alternative to waiting for NBC's taped transmission. But YouTube didn't exist when NBC bid for the television rights. What advice would you have given NBC? How do you make strategic decisions about the future that involve anticipating competitive threats from companies that don't exist at the time you have to make the decisions? As the French poet Paul Valéry is famously quoted: "The future isn't what it used to be."

In one recent survey, over 25 percent of CEOs said the lack of insight about customers in emerging markets constituted an obstacle to growth. Many U.S. and European managers have grown up in markets in which they were dominant and could set the rules. Now, given that more and more companies will be targeting more and more emerging markets, this statistic suggests that many leaders don't know their new customers as well as they should. And it implies that many aren't quite clear on how to get to know them.

Perhaps the most compelling uncertainty of all for CEOs is that their tenure is shorter than it has ever been. Those at the next level, the CEO's direct reports, are also more likely to leave after a short stay in their position. As a result, the most senior management team is often in flux. One CEO recently told us, "I know there is a bullet out there with my name on it." He meant that one negative event in financial reporting, one ethical lapse by another executive, one significant product recall, or pressure from Wall Street for better results could push him out of office.

In dramatically uncertain environments, leaders frequently make mistakes. One of the most common is overanalysis. Jimmy Carter was an engineer who became president of the United States, and like many leaders of his generation and background, was trained to examine data and be analytical. Unfortunately, Carter was overly analytical, and in the face of tremendous uncertainty, he was too cautious and slow to make decisions. Another president, George W. Bush, was a business school graduate whose mistake was just the opposite. He said he could not be bothered by details, analysis, and facts, and instead trusted his "gut" to make key decisions—including the ultimate decision to take his country to war. And in between these presidents was Bill Clinton, a president who could "feel your pain" but could not rationally and logically assess the risks of his own behavior. All three represent the potential derailment factors of overusing head, heart, or guts to respond to complex, ambiguous, and unclear situations, and we're seeing more and more leaders failing in this way.

When grappling with uncertainty, some leaders make the mistake of pushing decisions upstairs. Others become enmeshed in the data, trying relentlessly and often unsuccessfully to unscramble a mammoth helping of information and find some certainty in it. Still others opt for the close-your-eyes-and-point method of making a choice, ignoring the data and figuring that one decision is as likely to be right as another. Still others ignore all the data and just tough it out based on past experience.

Making decisions when uncertainty prevails requires guts. If you have a vision for your organization, knowing what you stand for and what you are trying to achieve, this perspective can guide your actions even when question marks abound. Clarity of vision makes it easier to navigate unclear waters. But again, it's not enough to have guts. Leaders must use their head when dealing with uncertainty, especially when it comes to risk. While risks can't be eliminated, the odds can be managed. Whole leaders are highly knowledgeable about the risks they're encountering, and if their course of action proves too risky, they are aware of this and correct their course to reduce their company's vulnerability.

Heart can also prove valuable in managing uncertainty—strong relationships can provide a buffer against unexpected events. CEOs who build and maintain relationships have an ear to the ground; they are likely to hear that runaway train rushing toward them. They also are able to rely on people they trust and who trust them when everything is up for grabs; they can count on receiving honest feedback and the best ideas (rather than the ones people think their leaders want to hear).

Andrea Jung, CEO of Avon Products since December 1999, had led her company successfully for five years. She had refurbished a tired brand, expanded its global footprint, and delivered financial performance that delighted Wall Street. All this was accomplished while delivering on the promise of making Avon the "company for women" and delighting employees with her emotional as well as intellectual acumen and vision. Then in 2005 the company's performance decelerated across the portfolio in developed and developing markets. But solutions to the company's problems were not obvious, and it wasn't clear exactly what needed to be done. At a pivotal moment during that period, when the pressure to respond was at its peak, a colleague advised her to go home for the weekend and come in Monday morning as if she were a new CEO brought in to fix the business. In essence, she was advised to "fire herself" and start over again. She responded to this challenge with just the right combination of head, heart, and guts. She dug into the analytics to figure out what happened. She reached out to her executive team and employees to get their perspective and to engage them in developing the solution. But perhaps most important, she showed the courage to make tough decisions: delayering the management ranks of the company, bringing in new talent on her executive team, and changing her own role as CEO to get more deeply involved in the operations of the business. Now, three years later, the company is better equipped to deal with future challenges than it has ever been.

What then is a leader supposed to do? How can you ever know if you have sufficient information to make a decision? How can you determine if you have too much? How do you know if you really understand the needs of your people and your customers? When is it time to act despite the uncertainty that lies ahead?

Mindy Grossman is CEO of Home Shopping Network, a company that has experienced a dramatic turnaround under her leadership. In addition to taking the company public, she has hired a mostly new team, refreshed the product offering, and opened new Internet channels for sales and distribution. In the uncertain consumer environment created by the recent credit crunch, she focuses on managing uncertainty by significantly stepping up communication with employees, partners, and customers, building more cohesiveness in her leadership team, and using data and analysis to build a nimble, flexible organization that can quickly recognize new patterns and events and respond to them. She focuses on core strategies and simplifies her messages and priorities to the organization, while emphasizing better decisions made lower in the organization. In a tumultuous environment of declining disposable income, fewer companies going public, and intense competition, HSN is navigating the storm and continuing to attract new customers and grow revenue.

THE IMPLICATIONS: WHAT WE NEED TO KNOW AND DO

Perhaps now you better appreciate our perfect storm metaphor. As the preceding examples suggest, leaders have never had to deal with the range and depth of issues they currently face. It's surprising that more leaders don't lose their way given the ferocity of their environment.

Yet a perfect storm can be navigated. Our descriptions of the complexity, diversity, and uncertainty trends are meant to foster awareness and understanding, not fear and trepidation. As challenging as it is to be a leader in the current environment, it is also possible to thrive. To do so, however, you must understand the impact of the dramatic trends in the external environment and develop leadership skills that allow you to deal with their impact effectively.

But understanding complexity, diversity, and uncertainty is not enough. You need to develop whole leadership skills to manage these issues successfully. Most of today's leaders developed through schools and training processes that never took whole leadership into consideration. Most business schools and executive education programs focus on developing head skills, and most organizational development processes emphasize cognitive competencies such as strategic planning and analysis. Other groups may help develop people skills and facilitate self-awareness. However, segmenting training and development in this manner prevents leaders from being able to use any or all of these three types of capabilities as situations dictate.

Every week we conduct senior executive leadership programs around the world with companies such as McDonald's, Nike, Novartis, Sun Microsystems, Disney, and many others. We have the chance to listen to executives who face complexity, diversity, and uncertainty discuss how they manage them. We've also interviewed twenty CEOs, presidents, and senior leaders for this book, and from all these conversations nine top challenges and responses keep appearing—things leaders have told us are at the top of their list every day, in one form or another. We believe these nine actions are critical for leaders who want to survive and thrive in the perfect storm. And for large, global companies, these nine steps comprise a new enterprise model of leadership.

If you are responsible for any part or all of a major company today, focusing on all nine of these actions will make you a successful enterprise leader. In each of the next nine chapters, we describe the leadership challenges and responses in depth, including how you can use your head, your heart, and your guts to become a whole leader and address complexity, diversity, and uncertainty in a holistic way. We think of this list as life rafts you can grab onto in the perfect storm we've described. Remember, there are no quick fixes—but there are some actions you can take, "whole leadership skills" you can put into practice to make yourself a better leader. We begin with the skill of destroying and then rebuilding your business model.

PART
TWO

**Nine Ways to Navigate
the Perfect Storm Through
Whole Leadership**

Section One: Navigating the Wave of Complexity

THE FIRST WAVE OF THE PERFECT STORM IS COMPLEXITY. During the last half of the twentieth century the world became more complex through the application of technology to virtually every aspect of life. With faster and faster technology came speed across the board, and the winds of change built up to hurricane force.

It is speed plus complexity that makes this first wave so challenging. Not only are industries changing, they are changing rapidly. Not only is the political, social, and economic landscape reconfiguring, it is reconfiguring at breathtaking speed compared with the move from a colonial to a postcolonial world after World War II. And businesses are redefining their profit assumptions, innovation processes, and organizational structures to catch up.

In this section we discuss the way whole leaders use their head, heart, and guts to navigate the complexity wave of the perfect storm. In Chapter Three we review how leaders are dealing with difficult competitive issues by destroying and rebuilding their business models. In Chapter Four we describe the way many leaders are now trying to focus, simplify, and network their structures to enable them to navigate more easily through the storm. And in Chapter Five we show how leaders can create an organization climate that enhances innovation.

CHAPTER 3

Destroy and Rebuild
Your Business Model

NOT TOO LONG AGO, THE IDEA OF DESTROYING AND REBUILDING your business model would have been considered a radical once-in-a-lifetime event that only a few leaders had to deal with. Today, more than half of leaders surveyed believe their current business model is flawed, often fatally. Anyone observing leaders of the auto or banking industries asking the U.S. Congress for financial assistance can grasp that old ways of doing business are not easy to change. In a recent study of six hundred U.S. corporations conducted by the Corporate Executive Board, it was predicted that 87 percent would hit what they call a "stall point"—a multiyear, significant downturn in revenue growth. Whether these businesses will see their current business model collapse tomorrow or ten years from now is uncertain. What is known, though, is that most business models probably were not built for a complex, diverse, and uncertain world. The perfect storm that has swept over organizations has rendered formerly well-designed models unseaworthy. If it were just a minor storm that we were dealing with—if, for instance, things had simply become a bit more complex—then the old model might have remained viable. It's the volatile confluence of significant complexity, diversity, and uncertainty, however, that makes it necessary to question every business assumption—and make changes accordingly. To remain competitive, business leaders are going to have to develop their capacity to destroy and rebuild their business models.

Before suggesting how to do so, we need to define our terms.

WHAT IS A BUSINESS MODEL, AND WHAT DOES CHANGE DO TO IT?

Every business has a *model*—essentially, the way in which the business is designed and conducted in order to serve and make a profit from customers. One of our colleagues, Adrian Slywotzky, has described a business model in his book *The Profit Zone*, consisting of five key elements: (1) which customers you decide to serve; (2) how you can continue to serve those customers, or sustain your business; (3) strategic control, or how you can exert some control in the marketplace; (4) what assets and activities you need to be successful, and (5) organizational architecture, or how you put together people, processes, structure, and leadership to be successful.

Any business design or model is temporary. Some may last longer than others, and in very stable industries they can last for many years. But in increasingly complex and uncertain times, business models are exceedingly temporary. Change happens unexpectedly,

FIGURE 3.1. *Elements of a Business Model.*

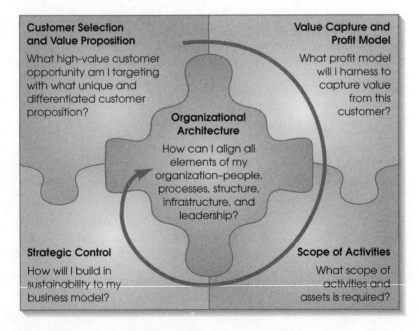

Customer Selection and Value Proposition	Value Capture and Profit Model
What high-value customer opportunity am I targeting with what unique and differentiated customer proposition?	What profit model will I harness to capture value from this customer?

Organizational Architecture

How can I align all elements of my organization–people, processes, structure, infrastructure, and leadership?

Strategic Control	Scope of Activities
How will I build in sustainability to my business model?	What scope of activities and assets is required?

and these are the times that test a leader's ability—and courage—to navigate through the storm. Nokia moved from a lumber company to a high-tech company over a hundred years, and in the process reinvented its business model numerous times. At crucial points, it was fortunate to have leaders who understood the need for radical change by redefining their business model—and even the industry they were in. This enabled the company to migrate into new industries that had greater future potential.

Obviously, changing industries is the most radical form of change. Most companies remain in the same industry, but reinvent the way they do business. Western Union is a great example of a company that survived severe disruptions by never confusing the business it was in with the way it did business. At its core, Western Union is about facilitating person-to-person communications and money transfers. It has learned to adapt to accomplish this from telegraph to wireless networks, phone, and the Internet.

Given that the success of any business model or approach is temporary, why do companies and leaders so strongly resist changing their model? Why do auto, steel, airline, telephone, and media companies need to experience wrenching change before recognizing that their model must be rebuilt? Why does it take the loss of market share, capital, and thousands of jobs before they act? Quite often the answer is leadership, or the failure to lead. The conclusion of the study by the Corporate Executive Board noted earlier was that leaders need to be able to reinvent their "mental models" in order to reinvent their business model. In other words, the first step in the process of reinventing your business is to understand that you have to move beyond many of the assumptions and beliefs you have developed about your business and your industry. This is not purely a head exercise, though the word *mental* would give you that impression. It is also a guts exercise, because it means making yourself vulnerable and taking risks that are enormous. Since few people have the courage to do this alone, heart also enters the picture in that you need to find some people who can take the risks with you and support you in the process.

Reexamining a business model is a challenge that often causes people to say yes—but achieve little. Most large companies have huge fixed costs tied up in the current business model, and to destroy it requires a leap into the unknown that their leaders are unprepared to make. They lack the guts to destroy it, but they also may lack the analytical skills to know when and how to destroy it and what to replace it with. And they may also lack the heart to help their people make the transition from an old, comfortable model to the new and uncertain one. And if that's not enough, the complexity, diversity, and uncertainty of the world raises the degree of difficulty another notch or three. Just when you've decided how to destroy the old model and what to replace it with, an unpredictable event or unforeseen complication is apt to send you back to the drawing board. Being in the center of a huge storm means that new waves come at you out of nowhere—economic, technological, and social waves that can make all your new model construction obsolete.

Though it may be more attractive to tinker with your current business model than to destroy it, for many leaders today that is not an option. Remaining competitive in a fast-changing world requires you to constantly think the unthinkable and be willing to do the unreasonable.

A GREAT MODEL FOR A WORLD THAT NO LONGER EXISTS

Nowhere is the new competitive world better defined than in China. The Chinese, after years of inward concentration, are now going global—and challenging many businesses elsewhere to rethink their business models.

Chinese companies are starting to disrupt global competition by breaking the established rules of the game—the Western game. Their weapon of choice has been cost innovation, the strategy of using Chinese cost advantage in radically new ways to offer customers around the world more for less. Galanz, a leading Chinese manufacturer, now supplies more than half of all microwave ovens sold on the global market. China International Marine Containers dominates the global container market with a 55 percent share, and Shanghai Zhenhua Port Machinery Company has 54 percent of the world market for cranes.

The response from Western companies to this competitive challenge cannot be incremental improvement or tweaking current strategies. They will need radical new approaches that will require them to drive their own costs down, or possibly even use their China business unit as a global product center.

In the United States and Europe, pharmaceutical companies once enjoyed a terrific business model—one that produced superior, predictable revenues year after year. The model required deploying a number of sales representatives into doctors' offices to educate physicians about a compound and secure their allegiance to prescribing it. Each year produced an increase in the number of sales representatives, since pharmaceutical companies could accurately estimate how much additional revenue each new rep would generate. As the Internet began to change how doctors obtained information, however, and a glut of sales representatives began to clog medical offices, doctors gave reps less than one minute to make their pitch. Today, pharmaceutical reps are operating at about 8 percent efficiency.

Pharmaceutical companies are caught—they recognize that they have to do things differently, but they are scared that if they eliminate half their reps, they'll never be able to replace the lost revenue.

The banking industry has gone through similar transformations over the years and now it is being challenged with reinventing not only its business model but its operating model as well as it moves into emerging markets. Barclays is a classic example.

Faced with limited growth in the U.K. market and exploding opportunities in emerging markets, Barclays decided in 2003 to reorganize its operations from a company of national operations in many different countries around the world to an integrated global enterprise that now serves 27 million people in a unified way. To do this it set a clear vision of profit growth through diversifying its business base. This meant the invention of new products and processes relevant to local markets, while employing a universal banking model that integrated the many disparate models that had been used locally around the world. Barclays management had to establish a single online interface globally to make it easy for customers to do business with the bank, regardless of where they were in the world. And to achieve this they had to reinvent relationships between various retail banking units, including the decentralization of many decisions to the lowest level.

Name any other industry and you'll find a business or operating model that is in need of replacement. The U.S. auto industry is another classic example of a business model that will require profound change. For decades, industry leaders could anticipate rising costs and greater competition for fossil fuels, fuel economy standards, climate concerns, and population density. But why face the difficulties of changing for tomorrow if customers were still buying SUVs today? Their risk-aversion, lack of vision, entrenched culture, and ingrained labor relations tension created the perfect context for precipitous decline. As Asian competitors competed on price and quality, U.S. auto companies made their money from financing—but with the current credit crunch, they need to figure out how to make money from actual vehicles, and not the traditional gas-guzzling cars but more fuel-efficient, greener modes of transportation.

The publishing industry is facing falling newsstand sales, subscription rates, readership, and ad revenue. Newspapers and magazines can see the future, and they are attempting to make the transition from print to digital platforms. Yet despite the writing on the wall—or the computer screen—they cling to their print publications and fail to destroy their old model.

Why? Part of the problem is one we alluded to earlier—they have a huge financial investment in the current model. Perhaps the more significant investment, though, is psychological. Many organizational leaders grew up with the old model; they saw it deliver great results year after year. It was the model that they learned well and that helped boost their careers. Destroying it feels wrong. It is counterintuitive to kill the golden goose—or the one that once was golden. And then there's the issue of how and when to kill it.

One recent study by Lahiri, Perez-Nordtvedt, and Renn concludes that to stay ahead of global developments and lead companies in a truly anticipatory fashion leaders need to develop four mind-sets:

- A global mind-set to understand worldwide market dynamics.
- An innovation mind-set to foster the generation and integration of new ideas into organizational strategy and business models.
- A virtual mind-set to incorporate the skills and knowledge of external providers who may be thousands of miles away.
- A collaborative mind-set that seeks out business partnerships to meet hyper-competition.

Destroying a business model and building a new one is intimidating if leaders lack these mind-sets and are unused to thinking broadly and innovatively. Leaders naturally ask themselves, Can we survive the transition from old to new model; do we have the people we need to implement the new model; what if things change and the new model is outmoded by the time we implement it? In these questions, you can see the complexity and uncertainty that give every leader pause. In many instances, they deny or delay the changes they know they need to make. They tell themselves that it isn't as bad as it appears; that perhaps there is some life left in their old strategies; that they can cut costs to keep their margins even if their revenue growth is lagging.

This is bet-the-company stuff, so all the rationalization is under-standable. But it's also unacceptable. As difficult as it is to destroy old models and build new ones, it is one of the crucial leadership tasks of the twenty-first century. Of course, you can find a million bad reasons for not blowing up your business model that seem reasonable at the time. It's worth examining some of the most common ones to see how they seduce leaders into inaction.

WHY IT'S WORSE TO DO NOTHING, BUT SEEMS TO BE BETTER

Why aren't CEOs and senior executives at least rethinking—if not destroying—their business models left and right? From our experience in working with top teams, here is what we've found:

Denial. Richard Tedlow notes that Sigmund Freud described denial as a state of "knowing-but-not-knowing." Leaders in this state refuse to believe what their analysis tells them. Confronted with the reality of a fatally flawed business model, they close their eyes to what it means for their companies and their careers. This isn't usually done consciously. In their day-to-day business lives, these leaders believe they are doing the right thing for their organizations and that they'll be fine if they simply stay the course. In the back of their mind, though, they glimpse the need for major change. They are generally able to keep this view buried in some dusty corner of consciousness and maintain the status quo. Many companies that are doing well today may be on their way to disappearing. Tedlow notes that according to economist Paul Ormerod, more than 10 percent of all companies in America disappear each year. And denial is a major reason.

Don't know what to do. Other leaders see the trend coming that will make their model obsolete, but they simply aren't sure what to do about it. The U.S. oil industry is an example. For all its windfall profits in recent years, it is finding that oil exploration and production has become more of a political than geological issue. "This is an industry in crisis," noted an energy expert in the *New York Times,* August 19, 2008: "It's a crisis of leadership, a crisis of strategy and a crisis of what the future looks like for the supermajor oil companies. They are like a deer caught in the headlights. They know they have to move, but they can't decide where to go." They lack a vision for how the company might reinvent itself, even knowing that fossil fuels will run out and consumers will conserve or demand alternative energy sources. So they scramble back to the United States to support off-shore drilling where they can have political access to supplies.

Lack of capacity to get where they want to go. Some CEOs have a clear point of view about how they must recreate their businesses, but they are missing the resources to do so. Perhaps they lack the money or the people, but they know that as their company is currently configured, they can't get there from here. Sometimes they have a conscious strategy of "finishing their term" in hopes that their successor will have the energy and the time to take the radical steps needed.

Stuck in the middle. Sometimes they start destroying the old model and start implementing the new one, but unexpected events cause the effort to grind to a halt. Everything from a competitor's move on a market or a downturn in the economy can cause leaders to find themselves unable to move forward. As a result, they move backward and restore the old model.

Relationship risks. Leaders are used to relating to their people in certain ways. For years, they've asked their people to do what is feasible and what jibes with a clearly stated direction. They have an unstated pact with their people—a pact that says I will only ask you to do what is reasonable and feasible; I won't ask you to attempt the impossible or the unimaginable.

Yet when leaders recreate companies and trash old business models, they often need to ask their people to do things that seem impossible or even crazy. As a result, making these requests gives them pause. They don't want their people to think they're idiots. They don't want to convey the impression that the business is in trouble or that they themselves are. In short, they don't want to endanger the emotional bond they've built over the years with key direct reports. Therefore, they often don't ask enough of their people. Rather than demand they throw out a long-standing process or discard an established policy or replace old products with new ones, they request minor rather than major changes. In this way, they preserve their relationships . . . at the expense of the business.

Blinding arrogance. Under the huge strain of witnessing the old model falling apart, some leaders are vulnerable to their derailers. Under stress, they reflexively resort to the worst aspects of their leadership personalities. For many leaders, their derailers involve arrogance. Faced with unrelenting pressures for improved performance from a tapped-out model, more than one CEO has decided to man the barricades and create a siege mentality. Arrogant, they believe that they're smart enough to solve their own problems without anyone's help. They hunker down with their key people and brainstorm solutions. Instead of destroying the old model and inventing a new one, they tinker with what they have in the arrogant belief that if everyone puts their heads together and tinkers with the model, they can make it work again.

Scapegoating others. While some leaders respond arrogantly to the stress of an outmoded business model, others become dismissive of their people, saying (or thinking), "I've got a bunch of imbeciles here. Why can't they give me the answers I need? I'm paying them to provide me with solutions, but all they do is raise problems." As a result, their people rather than their old business model become their focus. They may even replace their old people with new ones instead of replacing the old business model.

To counteract these action-stopping factors, you're going to have to find your way through the complexity. Here is how whole leadership thinking can help.

IT'S NOT JUST ABOUT GUTS: A WHOLE LEADERSHIP APPROACH TO DESTROYING AND REBUILDING YOUR BUSINESS MODEL

Joseph Schumpeter, an economic historian writing in the last century, firmly believed that the process of innovation required for economic development demanded the "creative destruction" of the current order on a regular basis. Without this, he concluded, there could be no economic progress.

Massive complexity and widespread uncertainty, of course, give leaders pause as they contemplate this process. Destroying a business model in a calm environment is difficult enough; in an environment where leaders don't understand everything that's happening and can't predict what's next, they naturally may hesitate. It's tough to take on challenging, risky assignments such as this one when you can't see clearly through the blizzard of change taking place.

In these stormy climes, leaders need a well-defined way to destroy their business models. The seven-step process we recommend requires a combination of head, heart, and guts, as can be seen in Figure 3.2.

1. *Use your guts to confront the reality of the current situation.*

First, you have to have the guts to confront reality and seek out bad news—something many leaders avoid. We are convinced that the reason leaders are looking for good news is that they are personally overwhelmed and so far into cognitive and emotional overload that they demand "positives" and "solutions" instead of problems from their subordinates. Confronting reality requires the guts to demand

---

FIGURE 3.2. *Destroy and Rebuild Your Business Model.*

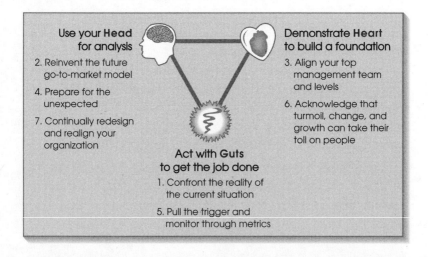

that people tell you bad news and then the head to analyze the results and determine what should be done. It also increasingly requires personal resilience to be knocked down by another unexpected event only to get up and lead your people in a confident fashion.

2. *Use your head to reinvent the future go-to-market model.*

Second, you need to reinvent the future. Arriving at a fresh point of view about the future from which a new business model can emerge may be the most difficult of the seven tasks. While the first one takes the courage to confront bad news, the second requires the analytical skills and vision to see new opportunities while at the same time sorting through the feasibility and financial impact of radical change. More than that, it's also necessary to hold together a team that may be frightened by the prospect of losing their tried-and-true ways of growing the business. But in the end, it may also call upon the guts to go beyond what is logical and rational to the unthinkable.

3. *Use your heart to align your top management team and levels.*

Third, develop alignment and support. This begins with your top team. You absolutely need to be sure your top team is on board and aligned with what needs to be done. This is first and foremost a heart issue of building successful relationships. But it may also be a guts issue of confronting resisters and ensuring that they get the message and understand that if they continue to resist, they'll be terminated. While your team may have been involved in confronting reality and developing a new business model, that does not mean they are aligned and supportive of the conclusion. You cannot, however, allow passive resistance and other dysfunctional group behavior to stand in the way. To ensure everyone is aligned, hold an offsite meeting in which you test and retest not only the conclusions you have come to but the degree to which people are on board and support the outcome.

Alignment extends beyond your top team to their direct reports. For this, you will need to hold your top team's feet to the fire; they must be accountable for ensuring that the next layer of management does not defect when times get tough. In some cases, you may need to offer to meet with this group to make the business case for the actions you are about to take.

Ken Frazier, president of Merck Global Human Health, is leading Merck's effort to change from an old business model to a new one. He recognizes that this transition is scary, and that people are dealing with questions of complexity that require continuous dialogue.

This means his leadership team needs to be open, honest, and effective. If people don't express their fears, listen to each other, and offer ideas and support, the transition won't be successful. For this reason, he spent three days a month for several months with his team to talk about the challenges, develop a shared vision of the future, make tough trade-off decisions, and find ways to support each other as the change goes forward.

Frazier grasped that reconfiguring a model requires continuous emotional support, not just analysis. He knows that members of his team are hearing their people tell them that they must be crazy to change the old model and that they're risking the business. Without sufficient support and a "we're all in this together" feeling, it is difficult for a team to move forward into implementation with the enthusiasm and conviction needed to be successful.

4. *Use your head to prepare for the unexpected.*

Fourth, you will need to prepare for the unexpected. Anyone who has ever sailed through a raging storm knows that contingency plans are critical. You may have one route mapped, but given the roiling, fast-changing conditions, you may have to opt for a secondary or tertiary route. Therefore, you must anticipate the major things that could go wrong and develop contingency plans for how they can be managed.

5. *Use your guts to pull the trigger and monitor through metrics.*

You have to do what was once unthinkable. You eventually have to push the button that blows up what you've worked hard to build. Maybe you do it in stages and maybe you use a euphemism to moderate the reaction to your program of radical change, but it still requires enormous courage. This challenge is no place for wafflers and wimps. You must be convinced that what you're about to do has to be done. Second thoughts, doubts, and half-measures aren't allowed. This is where your point of view or vision becomes critical. When you have a well-informed point of view in which you believe absolutely, you can make the tough decisions to initiate huge change with conviction.

Clear metrics will help you chart your progress in diagnosing what needs to be done, and then in measuring your progress once a new model is in place. Market share, customer satisfaction, new product introductions, turnover—whatever is critical to your success must be defined. Many leaders who are comfortable with the "big change picture" bypass the metrics needed to execute well and change direction if needed, and that failure can doom the whole change process.

6. *Use your heart to acknowledge that turmoil, change, and growth can take their toll on people.*

Most significant business model changes require pain and evoke frustration, anger, and even grief. We have worked with many large companies going through transformational change, and the most significant impediments to progress are usually heart, not head. Fear, anxiety, fatigue, letting go, clinging to control—these are the emotions that underlie most resistance. During periods of significant change, we see in chat boards, change workshops, anonymous surveys, and even all-employee meetings the same issues from company to company. "Will I be all right?" "Will I be able to adapt to the future?" "Can I get on board?" Good leaders use their heart to acknowledge and not deny this basic reality of change management, and excellent leaders know how long to tolerate it before it begins to impede performance.

7. *Use your head to continually redesign and realign your organization.*

Many leaders believe that once they have decided on a new business model and reorganized the business they can begin to focus on growing and winning. The stress and turbulence associated with rebuilding a business frequently requires a chance for people to catch their breath, adjust to the new direction, and stabilize. This can be a missed chance to focus on new learning, adapting to new competitors, and changing course quickly. Most organizations and leaders don't get it right the first time, or even the second time. Customers are disappointed, people must be changed out, and churn is inevitable. As indicated, be understanding of the chaos you have created—but don't ever let up on the pressure to learn, change, and grow.

Whole leadership provides an avenue for effective action. In fact, blowing up your business model without whole leaders is suicidal. With them, you stand a decent chance of making a go of it. It takes a leader with multiple leadership capabilities to overcome the natural resistance to blowing up a formerly strong business model during turbulent times.

As noted at the beginning of this chapter, reinventing your business model will probably not be a one-time experience—so you will need to find a way to do it and begin to hone your whole leadership skills in this area. Rethinking and redesigning your business is now a prerequisite for leading, and you will need to use your head to decide, your heart to empathize with what you will put people through, and your guts to bring yourself to do it.

As you consider these seven actions, consider also the following whole leadership questions related to this challenge:

WHOLE LEADERSHIP QUESTIONS TO ASK YOURSELF ABOUT DESTROYING AND REINVENTING YOUR BUSINESS MODEL

Use Your Head
- What happens if you don't blow up your business model?
- Is your business making money in the space where it's operating? Is it making as much as it did in the past; can it make as much in the future as it is making now?
- What blips on the radar screen might turn into solid objects in the future?
- What emerging trends, events, and competitors might be a real threat to your business's existence at some point in the future?

Use Your Heart
- What is changing in the minds of your customers? What are they looking for from your company and companies like yours?
- Does your business have the talent to meet competitive threats not only today but five years from now? Does it have the talent to run the company you hope it will become?
- If you destroy your business model, how many of your people will come along for the ride—with enthusiasm, commitment, and creativity?
- Have you done a good job of educating your people about the need for radical change? Do they understand why it needs to happen? Have you made a good effort to create awareness about and enthusiasm for the new model? Are investors and bankers aligned with the new model?
- Can you understand and appreciate the change people are going through, including acknowledging the past while focusing on the future?

Use Your Guts
- Are you willing to do the unthinkable?
- Have you pushed yourself far enough? Have you explored all possible avenues of company vulnerability?
- Do you really know what the competitive landscape looks like, not only today but in the future?
- Have you confronted the fact that you may have people on your team who are unable to go where you need to go?

CHAPTER 4

Focus, Simplify, and Network Your Organization

I N A RECENT INTERVIEW THE CEO OF ASTRAZENECA, DAVID Brennan, observed that in any large, complex organization, decision making becomes geometrically more difficult. One way he deals with this is to get senior and middle managers to focus like a laser on value creation. He believes that if his employees ask, every day, "What are we here for?" and "Is this action contributing to shareholder value?" some of the complexity in decision making can be reduced.

Brennan has found one of the answers to organizational complexity—focus—but most leaders today have found that everything has become more specialized, more sophisticated, and more technology-enabled—and more fragmented. The deeper they can delve into market segmentation, for instance, the better they can understand cost structures and the faster they can manage, track, and monitor performance. At the same time, the deeper they delve, the more likely they are to become buried in detail and lose sight of the bigger picture. Brennan points out that with the geometric increase in scale and scope come more people, more intersections of objectives, ideas, and decisions, and more opportunities to fail or succeed.

COMPLEXITY OF ORGANIZATION
SIZE AND SCOPE

Many of the leaders we interviewed told us that the increase in the number of relationships they have to manage is one of the most overwhelming aspects of leading their organizations today. New markets, new businesses, new regulatory bodies, and new partners require them to consider many more perspectives when they make decisions. At the same time, while more difficult to manage, these new networks are increasingly necessary because you cannot get things done in a complex organization without a network of people on whom you can depend.

But there are circles within circles. With the identification of different needs comes the possibility of over-identification. Paul Colby, CIO of British Airways, calls this "bad complexity." He notes that in the 1990s British Airways became so customer responsive that it offered millions of airfares to meet different market needs. In fact, it even had a special fare for dogs in boxes going from London to Budapest! When challenged by Ryanair and other discount carriers, it engaged in something it called "snapback," in which it started with what a simple airline looks like and then added layers of complexity that people would pay for. They found that the answer to their complexity was to "simplify."

CENTRALIZATION AND
DECENTRALIZATION

Over the last ten years the move to decentralize and simplify large organizations has been proposed as the best way to overcome the delays and complexity of approval and coordination processes stretched across thousands of miles. From Percy Barnevik's legendary decentralization of ABB into twenty-five hundred different businesses, each with its own P&L, to attempts today to push decisions down as far as possible toward the customer, leaders have looked for ways to speed decisions critical to market competitiveness.

At the same time, such moves have their parallel problems—too much decentralization can result in a lack of consistency and quality that can threaten global brands. The classic difficulties of power, authority, and control also arise. One CEO we interviewed recently told us that when people in his company say they want to be "entrepreneurial," they often mean they want to be autonomous. They want to go their own way to satisfy the demands of their local market while ignoring the needs of the total organization on a global scale.

Achieving the right balance between centralization and decentralization often translates into a structure where customer issues are managed locally and non-customer issues are managed globally. Johnson & Johnson has historically been decentralized and considers it a key operating principle. J&J is experimenting with ways to standardize nonessential core processes such as payroll and purchasing while maintaining the benefits of decentralized decision making around customers and markets. In this way, economies of scale and quality of support services can dictate the decision criteria for the back end while customer responsiveness dominates the decisions on the front end. This hybrid solution, however, increases the level of complexity and degree of ambiguity to be managed.

The greatest source of conflict for many organizations is in new product development, design, features, and packaging. Global franchises capture the benefit of global scale in manufacturing, but local markets often insist on unique features, language, or positioning. In most global companies this sparks conflict, debate, and sometimes ongoing frustration. Burberry recently decided that all products would be developed globally after experiencing quality and brand problems with local "entrepreneurs" in Asia. At the same time, Burberry CEO Angela Ahrendts wants to keep the local "entrepreneurial magic" while simultaneously ensuring the benefits of global branding, new product development, and strategic prioritization.

An emerging area of organizational complexity is the need to capitalize on the convergence of technologies, which often creates new organizational dilemmas. Converging technologies—drugs with devices, telephony with entertainment, media content with channels—require organizational units to collaborate and transcend individual or unit goals and budgets to work on a larger enterprise-wide objective—where, too often, the prize of technological convergence is visible but not achievable because of internecine warfare. Technology convergence will drive even more interdependency in the near future.

What's the Problem?

A large part of the problem is that most leaders try to outthink complexity. They deeply believe that if they can just figure out how to restructure the organization correctly, they'll have their product or marketing conflicts solved. But even if they solve one problem, another invariably surfaces (often as a result of solving the first problem). You may find a way to integrate multiple stakeholders into the decision-making loop, but this integration slows decision making down to the point that you can no longer decide fast enough.

While there are many reasons for organizational complexity, ironically, one of the most prevalent has been the emergence of what many consider a solution—the matrix organization. Unilever, Nike, Shell, GE, Tata, Infosys, Bank of America, and Novartis are all major global corporations that have opted for a matrix organization to deal with the simultaneous demands of local customers, global consistency, and business and product profitability. Yet just as it feels like an appropriate response to these complex factors, it embeds greater complexity into organizational structures. A different view of success is required to lead effectively in a matrix. Historically, the metaphor for organizations has been "the machine." Organization charts depict fixed relationships, static parts, and linear decision processes. This is the organizational "picture" many people unconsciously carry. The emerging and more accurate metaphor for organizations today is "the organism," which captures the ever-changing nature of organizational relationships, especially in a matrix.

Ever since Tom Peters and Bob Waterman wrote *In Search of Excellence* in 1982, a debate has raged about complexity and simplicity in organization design. Peters and Waterman maintained that of all the successful organizations they studied none was a matrix and most were single-focused. Yet the growth of complex global, multi-branded matrix organizations over the last twenty-five years has shown that some companies can manage scale, scope, and complexity simultaneously.

No one who knows anything about the human condition would ever design a matrix structure for organizations. And yet any organization that fails to do so probably won't survive in the long run. Most global companies today have evolved toward some form of matrix. But the result has been to create conflicting points of view about everything from measurement systems to control issues to who gets credit and rewards.

This conundrum perplexes leaders who are well aware that many of their employees have experienced command-and-control structures—work, family, or military—and frequently long for the clarity such structures provide. Within a matrix, however, authority is weakened, accountability is diffused, and many times people aren't even certain who the ultimate decision maker is. Nike probably has one of the most effective matrixes in the world and the most skill in managing it, but even there, employees can struggle with issues of accountability as they move from a product-based matrix to a category- and consumer-driven matrix structure. In short, a matrix is a solid but imperfectly designed structure for sailing through a perfect storm. In ways it is an improvement on earlier structures designed for simpler times, and yet it can't always withstand the whirling forces of complexity, diversity, and uncertainty.

Having more than one boss. Moving from one boss to two or three requires a significant shift in perspective for most people. Frequently, it increases the level of personal responsibility and accountability they must assume because they must learn how to secure approvals from the right person for the right project—and how to keep the secondary or tertiary authority figures in the loop. They must also deal with animosity between these authority figures. They must scramble to secure approval for a project or to meet a deadline when one or more of these individuals can't be located. For leaders trying to orchestrate thousands of relationships like this, the task is daunting, creating disillusionment and sometimes despair. It requires an increase in communication and influencing skill that many companies assume is present, even when it is not. People cannot be expected to move smoothly into a multi-boss environment after spending years with a one-on-one relationship. Making the new relationships effective while continuing to tear down boundaries and structures is a complex challenge.

Misaligned goals. People want different things—and have different goals and responsibilities. Managers in various countries need to satisfy their customers in ways that are locally relevant. Managers in HR, Finance, and IT need to make sure they have state-of-the art best practices and move toward centralization to get everyone aligned. And business managers are obsessed with delivering products ahead of the competition at a margin that is acceptable to the shareholders. All three of these groups have legitimate concerns that an organization needs to deal with, but ensuring that everyone works together effectively across these differing needs is more than a head issue.

The inability to operate autonomously. Leaders accustomed to making decisions on their own, or who just prefer it that way because of personality or personal style, sometimes find it onerous to engage in the collaborative process of a matrix. When accountabilities overlap, tensions are created and questions are raised. If you're accountable for the same project as five other people—and you're all working on it in separate groups—do you have to consult all five to report progress, share results, or make a decision? The process feels slow. It can also bog down in discussion and disagreement between the parties who need to collaborate. In our work with global companies, we have found that a larger percentage of mid-level managers than top managers cite "unclear roles and responsibilities" as their major frustration. We suspect that when senior managers are not aligned, it creates havoc lower in the organization.

An inward focus. When roles and responsibilities are less well-defined and influence takes precedence over position power, people naturally wonder "who's up" and "who's down." Not only do people speculate on who is doing well, they can also become insecure about their own positions and become more political than they were in a traditional hierarchical structure. It seems odd that this would be the case in a more open, participatory, and boundaryless organization, but it happens frequently. Instead of turning their attention outward on the competition, people look at their colleagues and expend energy jockeying for position. And leaders waste time trying to douse countless brush fires.

Don't misunderstand why we raise these four points. We absolutely believe in the value of a matrix to foster innovation, provide for a greater diversity of opinion and better decisions, and enhance organizational flexibility. It would be naive, however, to think that these benefits don't come without a cost—the cost of complexity.

Multiple Stakeholders, Multiple Headaches

As we have noted, decision making is more confusing now than ever before. But it's not only the matrix that is making it confusing. For the last fifteen years or so, we've been moving away from traditional, specialized decision making. In the past, people specialized by function or geography, and specialist leaders were kings—they made the decisions for their areas and could usually do so unilaterally. Now, everyone must take various stakeholders into consideration before deciding. Shareholders, for instance, are now much better informed and organized. They can and will lobby to rid a company of a leader they believe is not as effective as it needs. Just as important, evidence of a leader's effectiveness is out there for the world to see. In an age of transparency and technology, you can't expect mistakes to be hidden or blunders to just go away.

Employees, too, complicate matters. They no longer are *cubicleized*. They connect with each other on chat boards and other online forums, share disappointments and problems, and are not shy about voicing their concerns. It's not surprising, then, that CEOs are growing more attuned to what employees will think about their decisions. Even ten years ago, they might not have been troubled by what their people thought of a strategic move or a policy change. Now, they are extraordinarily sensitive to their employees' views on certain subjects.

Of course, if you try to satisfy everyone, you satisfy no one. Whole leaders recognize that while they must understand the various positions of different stakeholders and network with as many as possible, they can't try to make everyone happy all the time. Instead, they must create a connection with various stakeholders, a bond of respect and trust. In this way, a given stakeholder who doesn't agree with a decision will still give the leader the benefit of the doubt. Leaders also must have the courage of their convictions. If stakeholders sense that a leader is wavering or is taking the easy way out, they'll pounce. A leader with a strong point of view isn't invulnerable, but having that point of view is what will make it possible to act.

MATRIX MANAGEMENT: A JOURNEY, NOT A DESTINATION

Nobody ever "gets the matrix right" and then relaxes. There is no such thing as the ideal matrix organization. Organizations adapt based on changes in the marketplace, demands of customers, and moves of competitors. As a result, matrix organizations are always shifting emphasis, renegotiating lines of authority, and centralizing, regionalizing, and decentralizing responsibilities based on management's analysis of what is needed to win in the marketplace.

Everything seems to become outmoded in an instant; new developments around the world cause organizations to rethink assumptions continuously; a lawsuit, an investigation by a government body, or a new law requires massive changes fast. Organizational complexity can come from just about anywhere at any time.

Asking a large global organization to move in a new direction is a hugely complex request. Leaders must deal with everything from long-term employees' clinging to old policies and traditions to communicating the directional change effectively to multiple stakeholders. General Electric has managed to change direction continually—and profitably—over the years. It has no compunction about getting rid of what is no longer working and trying something new. Jack Welch made huge changes to the structure, culture, and strategy of the company, and Jeff Immelt is making equally significant changes by focusing on scientific research and increased emphasis on marketing. A 2006 article in *Fortune* contains a terrific quote from Immelt: "Most people inside GE learn from the past, but have healthy disrespect for history." Implied in that quote are the head and guts of a whole leader: You use your mind to analyze past events, but you possess the courage to ignore them and try something new.

Given all these complexities, if you try to lead a matrix with a purely analytical focus, you're bound to fail. So many paradoxical and multilayered issues exist that if you try and slog through all of them, you'll get stuck. In the *Harvard Business Review* authors David Snowden and Mary Boone introduced the concept of the "Cynefin Framework." They explained that *cynefin* is a Welsh word that suggests the existence of numerous factors that influence us in ways we can't grasp. They differentiated the ordered world of fact-based management from the unordered world where fact-based management is ineffective. They advocate an alternative approach (pattern-based management) for handling "complex and chaotic contexts."

We agree. An alternative approach is necessary, one that is highly flexible. *Flexible structure* means different things to different theorists, but for us, it means having access to your head, your heart, or your guts as the situation demands.

WHOLE LEADERSHIP AND MATRIX MANAGEMENT: FOCUS, SIMPLIFY, AND NETWORK

Most managers try to deal with complex organizations using only their heads and soon become overwhelmed with complexity. It is just not possible to hold in mind all the factors affecting policymaking today. Successful global leaders follow a basic process—focus, simplify, and network. They develop relationships with as many people throughout the organization as they can, because they know that in a complex organization, people do things first for people they know and like. Building work and social networks across borders therefore becomes a key step that requires empathy, interpersonal skills, and all the other aspects of heart. In our experience, most large global organizations that look like matrix structures on paper are in practice complex webs of key relationships that drive decisions and outcomes. These relationships require building and maintaining trust, which requires heart.

Whole leadership offers a way to manage complexity. When you can deal with a matrix through building trusting relationships and by making instinctive, value-based decisions, you're not forced to analyze the unanalyzable. As outlined in our whole leadership approach shown in Figure 4.1, using head, heart, and guts is needed to successfully manage in a matrix organization.

1. *Use your head to focus on value-creating activities.*

Create the "wiring and plumbing" to ease the transition of leaders from a hierarchy to a matrix. As a leader, you'll need to identify those activities that create the most value for the organization and

FIGURE 4.1. *Focus, Simplify, and Network Your Organization.*

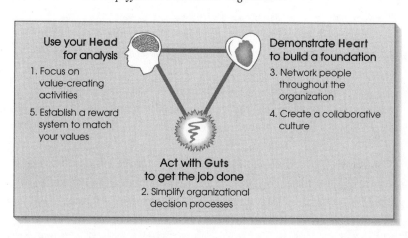

be ruthless in focusing on these priorities. After you've developed a business strategy and organization design to support it, you're ready to take action. Much like weeding a garden, identify the non-value-adding activities that take up time and energy in every organization—reports, approvals, meetings, sign-offs—and reduce or eliminate them. This work simplification process has been around for a long time, pioneered years ago by GE and termed "Work-Out" there. The point is to direct the organization toward those things that create value for the future, rather than just sustain the bureaucracy.

2. *Use your guts to simplify organizational decision processes.*

Once you have focused your priorities and reorganized or aligned your structure, simplify your policies and processes and relationships. This takes courage to make the tough decisions about the redistribution of power and authority. Mark Hurd, CEO of Hewlett-Packard, leads 150,000 employees in 170 countries—with a $55 billion supply chain. HP technology runs the world's top two hundred banks, twenty-five insurance companies, and hundreds of other companies. Hurd believed that the major source of complexity in HP was not size but the number of different countries and multiple businesses with different business models it had to encompass.

So he used a head approach. He reorganized the company to eliminate as many matrices as he could by pushing responsibility and accountability as low in the organization as possible. He then conducted an analysis of each country where HP was doing business and worked to align the organization to best meet local needs, while maintaining a global quality and delivery system. And finally, he required each manager to determine how much authority and responsibility would be given to global as opposed to local and regional units.

We know that mapping out how human relationships should work in a matrix can be enormously complex. We also know it's essential to make the effort. Consulting firms such as McKinsey have developed responsibility and accountability charts that can facilitate this effort, providing guidance so people can examine decision-making areas and determine who has the authority for certain decisions, who should be consulted, and who needs to be informed. While this renegotiation of power and authority is not easy, it helps to simplify what otherwise can be a totally confusing set of responsibilities for many day-to-day as well as strategic company decisions.

In an excellent article in the *Harvard Business Review,* Ron Ashkenas provides a wide range of practical suggestions for simplifying an organization. These include structural solutions like reducing levels and layers and increasing spans of control, simplifying products and services through phasing out low-value products, disciplining governance through streamlining decision councils and committees, reducing business processes by simplifying planning and budgeting, and simplifying leadership behavior through focusing on meeting management and interunit collaboration.

These are decisions and actions that require strong leadership and real guts, sometimes ignoring individual pleas and anxieties to achieve organizational success and outcomes.

3. *Use your heart to network people throughout the organization.*

To get any new initiative implemented in a matrix organization requires a network of relationships and a focus on trust. Think about what you're asking your people to do within a matrix. Many times, you're requesting that they take an action that is in the best interest of the company but may not be in their own best interest. You want them to depend on people halfway around the world to hold up their end of the bargain so they can get the bonus they feel they deserve. And you may require them to take time from their own daily responsibilities to help someone in another group achieve a goal for which they will receive little or no credit. As a leader, you must convince them that in the end, they will benefit from this sacrifice. People need to trust that the madness has a method in it, that they can trust their colleagues, and that ultimately they will be rewarded if they get with the new program.

Dan Vasella, CEO of Novartis, recognized this when Novartis moved to a matrix structure. We helped him develop and deliver a leadership program aimed at middle management that allowed leaders to examine four basic relationships they would need to manage if they were going to be successful. He stressed that they would need to learn to work across four boundaries—external boundaries with customers, suppliers, and regulators; horizontal boundaries between functional and business units; geographic boundaries between parts of the worldwide organization; and vertical boundaries between layers of the organization that inhibit quick implementation. More than two thousand middle managers have been trained to work across these boundaries, using 360-degree feedback on their leadership style and being coached on what they can do to become more effective in global matrix management. It has made a difference in the organization's acceptance of matrix organization and in its ability to operate in a matrix framework.

4. *Use your heart to create a collaborative culture.*

None of this, however, can take place without a highly collaborative culture. Collaboration has become the new mantra of matrix organizations. A recent IBM study of one thousand CEOs from around the world revealed that 40 percent are changing their enterprise models to drive more collaboration. When Dick Clark, CEO of Merck, decided to shift decision making from vertical functional and geographic authority structures to collaborative horizontal, end-to-end decision processes, he had to completely reassess his top 250 leaders to determine who could make the transition to a more collaborative leadership style and who could not, because he knew this would be critical to the organization's ability to implement its new organizational model. We worked with him to define the required leadership model and then assess key individuals against those requirements. It took both heart and guts to make this transition.

Dan Vasella and Dick Clark both understand the power of relationships to run a matrix organization. Managers who are unable to network and collaborate will inevitably fail in an organization structure that requires intense teamwork under complex, confusing, and uncertain conditions. Matrix organizations, more than perhaps any other type, require whole leaders at all levels.

5. *Use your head to establish a reward system to match your values.*

You also need to make sure your reward systems match your values. It does little good to preach trusting and collaborative relationships and then turn around and reward managers for silo behavior—especially if they are top managers in the organization.

One of the greatest challenges of any organizational culture change is ensuring that reward systems match the new desired leadership behavior. We have seen numerous situations in which leadership studies have been done to create a new model for future leadership. These models have been rolled out into the organization. People have been trained to operate in a new way—only to find that when they actually behaved in the new way, they were punished by systems that continued to reward the old behavior.

This kind of disconnect happens frequently in organizations that move from silo to collaborative behavior, because many of the silo managers are critical to the business, leading countries that have been mainstay markets, businesses that have been cash cow contributors, or functions that have been critical for business success. If these leaders are allowed to continue their old behavior patterns in a new collaborative culture, however, the credibility of the new culture is undermined, and the transition will never happen.

It takes focus and networking to ensure that new reward systems match the needed behavior—and that they stick.

WHOLE LEADERSHIP QUESTIONS TO ASK YOURSELF ABOUT FOCUSING, SIMPLIFYING, AND NETWORKING A MATRIX ORGANIZATION

Use Your Head (Focus)

- Is your organization clear about business priorities for the coming year and how these may be best achieved?
- Have you made a business case to your stakeholders about why the current matrix organization is necessary to meet your business priorities?
- Have you made clear the authority relationships between geographic areas, business units, and functional areas in achieving your business objectives?
- Do you have in place the necessary metrics to know when and where the matrix structure is working and where it may be creating unnecessary additional costs?
- Are IT and Finance prepared to provide the right information to the right people at the right time with the new organization structure and processes?

Use Your Heart (Network)

- What relationships do you need to establish to build deep face-to-face trust and ensure critical tasks get done?
- Who needs to understand the business case for difficult decisions that will be made, because you need their support?
- Who will most likely resist the decisions that need to be made? What are their concerns? How can you address these concerns in other ways?
- How do you provide support throughout the organization for the difficult transition?
- Have you led the way in developing a new leadership model and related assessment and performance measurements for the mind-sets, knowledge, and skills needed by managers to operate in a complex organization?

- Have you provided enough training and orientation to your managers about these mind-sets, knowledge, and skills for them to understand the new criteria for leadership?

Use Your Guts (Simplify)

- What can you do to align this organization's systems and core process around the most important issues for the future?
- What tough trade-off decisions will you be willing to make in increasing the speed of decision making for inclusion of all relevant stakeholders in policy decisions?
- How can you balance simplifying without sacrificing the key perspectives you need for quality decision making?

5

Build a Climate for Innovation

WHEN A. G. LAFLEY BECAME CEO OF PROCTER & GAMBLE IN 2000, he had his work cut out for him. Profits were lackluster and the stock price down. New product launches had slowed to a trickle, and no more than 15 percent of them were making money. He knew that fresh thinking was needed throughout the organization. Moving quickly, he cut jobs, sold Crisco shortening and other declining brands, and began reciting his mantra: innovate, innovate, and innovate. These days more than half of P&G's new products are commercially successful.

The increasing complexity of the competitive landscape is forcing every company to innovate faster. Judy Estrin, former CTO of Cisco Systems, has written in *Closing the Innovation Gap* that the United States is falling behind in innovation compared to other countries. Estrin argues that short-term focus, risk aversion among entrepreneurs, and regulations make innovation difficult for companies today. As in the pharmaceutical industry, a slowdown in new product introductions has left companies with oversized sales and marketing machines. Pricing pressures are increasing as companies globalize their operations while costs continue to climb. And old business and operating models are becoming outdated daily.

Most organizations respond to these pressures by focusing their innovative efforts on product and service offerings, followed by business processes, product and service delivery models, financial and business models, and developing new management mind-sets and skills—in that order. But observers increasingly believe that the lowest cumulative value creation over the last ten years has been on products and the highest has been on the type of reinvention of business models discussed in Chapter Three. Innovation applied only to product development is not the answer for the future.

As a leader, you know that mandating innovation isn't enough. How many times have you asked your leaders and your organization to innovate and found that little or nothing happens? You may find that your people respond with creativity—what Peter Drucker defined as the generation of new ideas—but that's different from innovation, a process that requires leadership. And not just any type of leadership. To catalyze innovation within a perfect storm is a major challenge. People are nervous about taking risks when things are highly uncertain and unclear, and they are so exhausted from trying to manage a diverse cast of characters that innovation is the last thing on their minds. During the tumult of a perfect storm, most people's instinctive reaction is to cling to what is known rather than come up with something different. In other words, organizations aren't going to stimulate successful innovation in this environment unless leaders operate at full and broad-based capacity. That's why we believe leadership—the whole variety comprising head, heart, and guts—is the most critical component of innovation.

In the end, innovation depends heavily on the organizational gestalt—a mixture of culture and climate. It consists of the company's stated and tacit rules of operation. It involves a clear-eyed look at everything from stated leadership policies to what is implied and intuited (see Table 5.1). When you think about this gestalt and how friendly it is to innovation, consider the following questions:

- How is innovation seen in your organization?
- Does R&D own innovation? Or does everyone feel a responsibility for driving innovation?
- Is the focus of innovation on new organizational processes, organizational cost cutting, and new market development—or all three and more?
- What do people think of when they hear the word *innovation?* Do they think of whether they are creative or do they think of whether they are responsible for thinking in new ways that create value for the organization every day?

TABLE 5.1. *Common Innovation Myths.*

Myth	Reality
Innovation is driven from the bottom up . . .	Effective innovation is leadership driven.
	Leaders create the innovation strategy and sustain innovation through their leadership practices.
Innovation is about big ideas . . .	Innovation is about all ideas that create value.
	Innovation ranges from sustaining or incremental to revolutionary and market changing.
Innovation is about investing in a hot new product . . .	The real payoff comes from investing in multiple types of innovation with an emphasis on business model innovation. New products are copied swiftly and rarely enjoy sustained profits.
Innovation starts in R&D . . .	Innovation can start anywhere. It requires a flexible and open framework that encourages new ideas and thinking.
Innovation comes from being creative . . .	Innovation is far likelier to come from being disciplined.
	There must be a clear process of transforming ideas into tangible outcomes.

As a leader, you are responsible for ensuring that your organization responds to complexity with agility and adaptability. To do that, you need to establish not only a culture that values innovation but a climate in each sector, division, department, and work unit that creates the conditions for organizational innovation. This means that leaders at all levels of the organization can manage the complexity of total organizational innovation by the way they lead their people. But how do you get leaders to create an organizational gestalt that leads to innovation? Much has to do with creating just the right climate at a time when the perfect storm encourages creating just the wrong climate for innovation.

A SIX-DIMENSIONAL APPROACH

We have developed a six-step model to help senior executives understand the requirements for building an organization climate that encourages innovation. Figure 5.1 sets out the basic components.

FIGURE 5.1. *Six Dimensions of an Innovation Climate.*

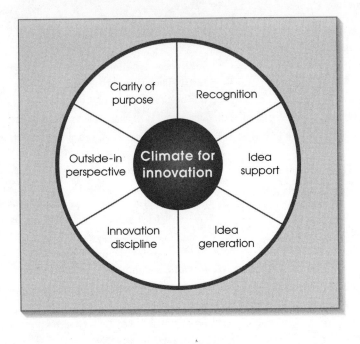

Here's a look at each one to spell out their impact on innovation.

Clarity of Purpose

The message you send your organization regarding innovation is vital. As noted earlier, people were clear that A.G. Lafley saw innovation as a critical answer to their problems. Your people have to have the sense that innovation is a business priority—for everyone—and that business success will depend on the development of new ideas that could lead to the big payoff—the "disruptive innovation."

But there also needs to be an innovation plan that provides guidance to people concerning how you expect them to innovate. One of the first steps in this process is to look outside the organization.

Outside-In Perspective

Encourage people to take an outside-in perspective. Customers, competitors, suppliers all have views on ways you can improve your organization—most of which you probably don't want to hear. Confronting reality, as many people have said, is the first responsibility of a leader.

When Steve Jobs took the stage for his first speech after returning to the top of Apple in 1997, he shocked everyone by saying that he believed that Apple would need to move outside of its own ecosystem and reach out to other partners for help. Jobs felt that Apple, which had prided itself on its internal innovation, had become isolated and forgotten the world in which it lived. He did not just ask people to be innovative, he gave them permission to find innovative ideas in ways that had not been part of the corporate culture. As a result, Apple moved from a sheltered tech organization to a global empire with more than 200,000 companies creating Apple-compatible products.

This approach, which has led Apple to become the integrator of technologies from around the world while adding its own value, has become known as "open innovation," and it is not limited to electronics. Lafley has developed his own version for product development at P&G, where it's called "Connect and Develop," and this radical strategy of open innovation now produces more than 35 percent of the company's innovation and billions of dollars in revenue. British Telecommunications (BT), several drug giants, and many other companies now assume that the bulk of their future ideas will come from outside. Making open innovation work means cultivating contacts with start-ups and researchers outside your organization and constantly scouting for new ideas—anytime, anywhere.

Remember that perfect storms tend to be blinding, and innovation opportunities outside the field of normal vision are often invisible to the searching eye. Imagine you're the captain of a ship, surveying a storm-tossed sea for a new route with only an old-fashioned spyglass to find your way, and then imagine you're equipped with radar, sonar, and night-vision goggles. In short, look everywhere for the best ideas, and develop the capacity to look outside your normal range of sight.

Innovation Discipline

Giving people an understanding of innovation as a priority, along with permission to go anywhere in the world to find the best ideas, are good first steps. Then you need to lay out a disciplined process for moving ideas into action. Coyne, Clifford, and Dye maintain in a recent article in the *Harvard Business Review* that it is not enough to tell people to brainstorm. Instead, they have developed a disciplined approach to brainstorming in which they narrow a question to force people to think in new ways. For example, they suggest asking questions like these: "Who uses our product in ways we never expected or intended?" "Who else is dealing with the same generic problem as we are but for entirely different reasons?" "What is the biggest hassle of purchasing our product?" and "How would we do things differently if we had perfect information about our buyers, usage and distribution channels?" In each case, the guidance for brainstorming transforms the process from total chaos to a more focused and disciplined exercise.

Develop an organizational process for identifying and implementing new ideas. This means that innovation needs to be coordinated across the company. In addition to his "open innovation" process, Jobs also created a "developer program." Through this process, the company worked with makers of portable speakers, music player cases, and other add-ons to greatly enhance the value of the iPod. Jonathan Schwartz, CEO of Sun Microsystems, blogs every day, and many of his blogs are about keeping innovation at the forefront of people's minds.

And transparency of information drives everything. In the senior leadership programs we conduct, we find that people are increasingly concerned about how to make their products, processes, and positions more transparent. Being transparent in a systematic fashion provides channels for people to contribute innovative ideas. Innovation can't exist without discipline, but the discipline cannot be control-oriented—it must provide room for individual thinking, collaborative networking, and idea generation.

Finally, innovation discipline also takes the guts to walk away from ideas that don't work. Many companies lose time and valuable resources because they don't know how to walk away from a failing project. Rapid prototyping, which allows an idea to fail fast and cheaply, can free up resources to go after ideas that can create real value for the organization.

Idea Generation

Iyer and Davenport report that Larry Page, Google's co-founder, after being told that an error was committed that cost Google several million dollars, said, "I'm so glad you made that mistake because I want to run a company where we are moving too quickly and doing too much, not being too cautious and doing too little. If we don't have any of these mistakes, we're just not taking enough risk."

Idea generation involves giving employees the sense that they are expected and encouraged to take initiative and create new ways of doing things. People should be encouraged to experiment and try new approaches, even if they involve a certain amount of risk. Google famously requires all engineers to spend 20 percent of their time pursuing their own ideas!

Getting employees to generate ideas, however, also requires leaders to clear as many bureaucratic obstacles as possible. How many times have you heard of a new idea or initiative that has languished in your decision-making infrastructure while different layers of management made sure that all risk was taken out—and in the process killed the initiative? As a leader, you need to let it be known that you do not expect perfect ideas, you expect numerous ideas for the company to experiment with.

Follow one of W. Edwards Deming's key points to manage quality: to get ideas to bubble up through the organization, you need to "drive out fear!" Deming, the father of the quality movement, maintained that no organization would be innovative or develop quality products and processes as long as a climate of fear existed that prevented people from being forthcoming. Debilitating fear can range from reluctance to be embarrassed or ridiculed in public to fear of being fired.

Support for idea generation must be provided on a personal basis—which is why the climate you and your managers set in your work units is so important.

We have found that one of the most difficult insights for leaders is how much impact they have on their subordinates. Most leaders feel they are open and understanding, full of empathy and concern for their people. They cannot understand why anyone would fear them or be hesitant to tell them what they are thinking. It is imperative to move past that comfortable belief and see what is really happening.

When you have power and authority over someone else's life, however, you are never "just another nice person." As a result, the recognition you give means much more than you think it does. Think about how you feel when someone you report to recognizes your good work. Now transfer that same feeling to the people under you—or even to a colleague who respects you and seeks your approval. You hold a tremendous amount of authority in whom you recognize and what you recognize them for.

And the power is not only over the person being recognized. You are also sending a signal to the rest of the organization about what it is you value. Be careful that you recognize those behaviors that will most support innovation and that you do not inadvertently reward and recognize people who are seen as resistant or "not on board." This message can undermine all your good efforts and create a negative climate for innovation.

Idea Support

Managers and their people must support the development and implementation of new ideas, and they must communicate that anyone who fails to support these ideas will be dealt with. While we've alluded to this idea previously, what we haven't looked at is how trust is the linchpin for such support. Much has been written about trust—from the organizational level to the interpersonal. There is universal agreement that trust is crucial to effective organizational performance and, in fact, is even more crucial today now that the success of most organizations rests increasingly on horizontal collaboration in addition to vertical specialized expertise. Stephen R. Covey maintains in *The Speed of Trust* that trust is a critical competitive weapon, because speed to market cannot be achieved without trust. He believes that low trust leads to hidden agendas, work duplication, poor communications, and interdepartmental rivalries that reduce the speed of decision making and therefore speed to market.

Many leaders today are finding that in a globally interdependent organization, a poor performer in one unit can undermine the ability of the whole organization to operate effectively. If you have an underperformer in your unit, it means that other units cannot have confidence in your consistency of performance—and there goes organizational trust.

The same is true within a unit—if you want your people to trust one another, you have to deal with poor performers. It is irrational to expect your people to trust those who are incompetent and inconsistent in their performance.

If people feel trusted and believe they will be supported, the challenge becomes establishing a climate where colleagues and direct reports can openly critique new ideas without leaders seeing it as a personal attack and source of embarrassment.

In the course of analyzing 360-degree survey feedback results of many senior leaders in companies throughout the world, we have seen that facing and handling conflict is among the poorest skills of most managers today. Yet conflict of ideas is at the heart of innovation. If people cannot critique one another's ideas openly for the purpose of improvement, they won't be innovative.

Finally, leaders must provide the resources needed to move a good idea forward. People today are so overworked and stressed out that they have no time for additional responsibilities and no resources for finding more help. In this kind of environment you may need to use your own knowledge and skills to provide some form of additional support so that important projects are prioritized. This means the allocation of time, capital, and structure to ensure that those with new ideas have the resources to implement them.

Idea Recognition

Recognition involves rewarding and recognizing your people for implementing innovative ideas. Or—for that matter—recognizing people for ideas that don't work, as Larry Page did at Google. Use recognition to encourage the behavior you want to support. Everything you do—from the amount of time you spend with someone to the resources you allow them to receive to the promotions you make or even the handwritten notes you might send home to congratulate someone on something they have done—offers leverage for innovation.

This is true for the team as well as for individuals on it. Any team needs to understand why and how and where recognition is given. The more transparent you are not only in your recognition but also in why you are recognizing a particular idea, the more you can use recognition as a coachable moment to help other people understand what you value.

MANAGING THE PARADOX OF ORGANIZATIONAL CLIMATE

To achieve all this requires balance—and the management of an interesting organizational paradox. As you can see in Figure 5.2, too much support and recognition of people can lead to a country club climate where all the emphasis is on people support—idea generation,

FIGURE 5.2. *Paradox in Organizational Climate.*

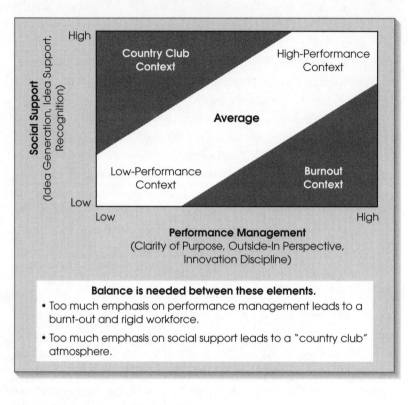

Source: Birkinshaw and Gibson, 2004.

support, and recognition. On the other hand, if you try to motivate people toward innovation only through organizational means—clarity of purpose, outside-in perspective, and innovative discipline—they will not have the personal support they need. Obviously, the answer is a balanced approach where performance management is mixed with social support.

You got it—you have to be a whole leader to succeed at innovation.

WHOLE LEADERSHIP APPROACH TO BUILDING A CLIMATE FOR INNOVATION

Leadership values and practices have the biggest impact on organizational climate. This, in turn, will affect employee motivation and

FIGURE 5.3. *Build a Climate for Innovation.*

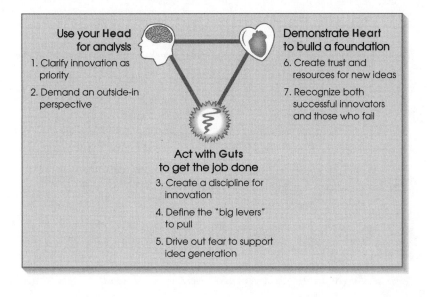

individual and team performance. To achieve a successful team climate, you need to use your head, heart, and guts. As can be seen in Figure 5.3, your head provides clarity of purpose and the outside-in perspective; your guts provide innovation discipline and idea generation; and your heart provides idea support and recognition.

1. *Use your head to clarify innovation as priority.*

As noted, your ability to communicate clearly to your organization in concrete terms, explaining how you see innovation related to your vision for the organization, is critical. This is not merely a matter of saying that it is important; you need to develop a clear innovation plan that lays out how you expect innovation to occur. What are the organizational processes, the managerial behavior, and the procedures for ensuring that innovative ideas will be successful?

2. *Use your head to demand an outside-in perspective.*

It is hard to demand an outside-in perspective from others if you do not step outside the organizational boundaries yourself. Customer visits, competitive analysis, industry meetings, and global travel are all steps that leaders take to make sure they are challenging their assumptions about their approach to the business. We work with many senior teams who incorporate the discipline of beginning their team meetings with this valuable perspective—rather than focusing on the past month's performance or the usual metrics. Adaptive organizations and leaders keep the focus on the external view, including incorporating the voice of the customer in creative ways to every meeting.

3. *Use your guts to create a discipline for innovation.*

People need to know the process for getting new ideas approved: who makes the tough choices; how to work through a resistant system; where political support can be found. They also need to know they can count on senior management to hold middle managers' feet to the fire and make sure that managers lower in the organization know they will be heard if they advance new ideas.

4. *Use your guts to define the big levers to pull.*

Most innovation in companies is driven by clear "levers" that accelerate the innovation process. These levers depend on the industry and the business, but might include aspects such as finance, networks, enabling processes, core processes, and product performance. Each of these are levers in the innovation process that require disciplined attention. Innovation leaders focus on the key levers, rather than all of them, to drive innovation in their particular business.

5. *Use your guts to drive out fear to support idea generation.*

You can develop every system and process for innovation you think would ensure success, but if people are afraid to come forward with suggestions and ideas for fear of ridicule or worse, innovation is dead. Many leaders have discovered that creating a climate for risk-taking, surfacing ideas, and exploring boundaries takes continuous work, suspending judgment (for a while), and creating conditions for people to speak freely, spontaneously and openly. Creative companies such as IDEO, W. L. Gore, and many advertising agencies shape all aspects of an organization to support idea exchange, including office layout, meeting design, and even play time. But we have found that the most critical factor in driving out fear is the behavior of the leader, especially in reacting to ideas that aren't immediately pleasing or easy to understand. Good leaders learn to probe, ask questions, and reiterate, rather than close down discussion for the sake of meeting efficiency.

6. *Use your heart to create trust and resources for new ideas.*

After driving out fear, building trust is the next step. It is one thing for people to be unafraid to raise new ideas; it is something else for them to feel a supportive and helpful climate in which to do so. Create a climate where people can feel mutual respect, have open, problem-focused discussions, learn how to deal with conflict and differences of opinion, and believe that everyone has everyone else's best interests in mind (and heart). This won't happen without some specific time devoted to building the team and its members' ability to work with one another. A key leadership behavior is to display some vulnerability, including the ability to say "I don't know" and "I'm learning, too."

7. *Use your heart to recognize both successful innovators and those who fail.*

Recognizing failure as well as success sounds good, but it can be tricky to put into practice. Developing parameters for where and when failure will be recognized is obviously a head issue, but putting yourself in the position of people who have failed and are trying to understand why they have failed and whether they failed from personal inadequacies or from circumstances beyond their control is very much a heart skill. Many leaders who conduct accountability investigations after failures are more concerned about attaching blame than about learning from the experience, and this blame can destroy all the good work they may have done to develop an innovative climate in their organization.

If all this seems an overly complicated way to go about innovation, welcome to the twenty-first century. In fact, what this head, heart, and guts approach represents is a relatively simple way to deal with the complexities of innovation. Creating an innovation gestalt is not rocket science, but it isn't as simple as issuing a proclamation that innovation is now the law of the land. As we hope you understand by now, the climate in your company is set by leadership head, heart, and guts. All three play roles, and to ignore one is to create a fatal flaw in your innovation strategy. To acknowledge and incorporate all three, on the other hand, offers protection against the terribly turbulent forces that cause leaders to seek shelter in the tried and true.

To determine your ability to create an innovative organizational climate, try the exercises described in the next section.

WHOLE LEADERSHIP QUESTIONS TO ASK YOURSELF ABOUT BUILDING A CLIMATE FOR INNOVATION

Use Your Head

- Do you communicate a clear vision and strategy for the business?
- Do you emphasize that innovation is a business priority by establishing a clear innovation plan?
- Do you encourage people to improve business processes as well as products and services?
- Do you make the identification and implementation of innovative ideas a top priority?
- Do you make decisions based on an in-depth understanding of customer expectations?
- Do you stay abreast of changing industry and market conditions?
- Do you insist that people share customer and market knowledge with others in the organization?
- Do you recognize the value of bringing together people with different opinions and points of view?

Use Your Heart

- Do you build high-trust relationships with people? Keep commitments?
- Do you conduct team meetings in a way that builds trust and mutual respect?
- Do you encourage an open airing of problems and differences of opinion?
- Do you seek creative ways to resolve conflicts?
- Do you reward people for their efforts to innovate, even if their ideas don't always work?
- Do you reward people for experimenting with new approaches rather than criticizing them for mistakes?
- Do you recognize and reward team performance as well as individual performance?
- Do you relate rewards to performance, rather than other factors such as seniority or personal relationships?

From heart we go to guts—once you have decided you have to innovate and have made the business case for it, you then need to have the guts to confront sacred cows and establish a disciplined process whereby innovative ideas are generated and supported. This will probably require going against the grain of the organization and in some cases may even raise questions with your direct reports and supervisors about your judgment. Perseverance here is key—based on a passionate belief that what you have discovered in the first phase of your analysis is critical to your future.

Use Your Guts

- Do you manage innovation efforts with relentless focus?
- Do you encourage people to share ideas and information with other organizational units?
- Do you make tough decisions when it comes to allocating resources?
- Do you develop thorough and realistic plans and processes for translating ideas into actions?
- Do you encourage innovation and calculated risk taking?
- Do you challenge people to consider alternative approaches?
- Do you give people time and resources to pursue innovation projects?
- Do you remove obstacles to innovation and the implementation of new **ideas?**

Section Two: Navigating the Wave of Diversity

THE SECOND WAVE OF THE PERFECT STORM IS diversity. It's not that diversity is new as much as that the underlying diversity of the world has been brought out into the open through technology. When the first commercial jetliner came into service in 1957, it changed the world. People could move quickly between markets, finding new customers, suppliers, and workers. The ability to conduct business globally grew slowly at first, because while aviation technology could take people places, computer technology had not yet made it possible to coordinate, consolidate, and integrate businesses on a global scale.

As computer technology became an enabler of faster and better global coordination and communication, and as the mature markets that had driven global growth became saturated, businesses began reaching out to the emerging marketplace of the 1980s and 1990s for new opportunities. They discovered, however, that these markets were different. They had different cultural values, different buying patterns, and eventually new competitors with different mind-sets and strategies. This diversity took many traditional companies by surprise. Suddenly leaders needed to reexamine their global business strategies, structures, and processes to determine how to meet a wide variety of totally unfamiliar needs and demands.

In the following chapters we examine three aspects of the diversity wave. In Chapter Six we discuss the emergence of market diversity. Chapter Seven covers the impact of cultural differences on global workforces. And in Chapter Eight we discuss global communities of interests as increasingly powerful stakeholders in companies throughout the world.

Leaders riding the waves of diversity in today's perfect storm without adequate knowledge of global marketers, workforces, and stakeholders do so at their own peril. But whole leaders use their head, heart, and guts to steer a steady course.

6

Differentiate and Integrate Your Markets

TECHNOLOGY DRIVES DIVERSITY, AND DIVERSITY PLUS TECHNOLOGY drive complexity and uncertainty. This should be every leader's mantra. Repeat it frequently and reflect on its implications. It suggests that organizations will not be able to respond to diverse global markets if they don't possess an integrated information technology that helps them learn about and communicate with rapidly differentiating communities of interest around the world. At the same time, the rapidly diversifying customer base is fueled by technology—customers in China, India, and elsewhere who learn about and develop aspirations for certain types of products and services via the Internet. And all this happens at warp speed.

The interaction of rapidly changing technology and increased global diversity means it is no longer possible to win today as companies have won in the past. For instance, you can't sell second-generation products in developing countries while creating and promoting third-generation products for your home country—or at least this strategy is less likely to work now than even a few years ago. Customers in Shanghai and Vladivostok no longer readily accept the old model; through the Internet, they know too much about the new model and aspire to have it just as soon as people do in developed nations. In addition, their standard of living may dictate a lower acceptable price point, required features that are unique to their environment, and customization and responsiveness to their own needs. Some call the West's continued attempt to sell old products and models "technological imperialism."

The old mantra was: Market to a diverse customer base and be responsive to different demographic groups. Following this old wisdom, however, has significant risks today. You'll end up trying to sell the same product to wildly different markets—and the product that works fine in one market won't do as well in ten others. Differentiation by market is critical, but integration is equally important for cost-effectiveness, driving global brands, and sharing best practices. The challenge for all companies involved in global markets is to somehow find the right balance between local differentiation and global integration.

The perfect storm metaphor is particularly apt here. When it comes to market diversity, the issues are tremendously uncertain and complex. The risk and uncertainty involved following the old wisdom of marketing to a diverse customer base is troublesome enough on its own, and this uncertainty is now merging with all sorts of mind-boggling complexities. One school of thought suggests that globalization is leading to convergence, rapidly eliminating differences in tastes and preferences. Others argue that this is nonsense and that cultural and national differences are even more important now as people attempt to differentiate themselves from mass marketing and retain their local identities. What makes this issue so complicated is that both points of view are correct, or at least partially so.

McDonald's is probably one of the world's most studied global companies. It has worked hard to achieve the right balance between globalization and meeting local needs: developing common standards for food preparation, kitchen layout, purchasing, supplier relationships, and customer service, while allowing local franchises to have different menus, product promotion, pricing, and public relations.

U.K.-based Vodafone has operations in twenty-five countries and 60,000 employees whose mix of nationalities reflects its global business. CEO Arun Sarin said: "Less than 5 percent of our operating profits come from the U.K. We've had to fundamentally redesign this company as a global company. In Germany, we feel German. In Italy, we feel Italian. In Spain, we feel Spanish. In India, we feel Indian. Here, we feel British. But there are [still] common values and common skills that we look for."

This blend of global and local brings to mind the transnational form of organization described by Chris Bartlett and Sumantra Ghosal some years ago. Successful companies, and leaders, have to find the right balance in a world where rapidly changing technology gives people instant access to information, and where diversity takes them into new markets. Of course, finding the right balance in a highly volatile, unpredictable environment is a huge challenge. Storms of the magnitude we're facing make it extraordinarily difficult to navigate the local-global balance. And navigating through a sea of rapidly moving values poses particularly fierce challenges for leaders.

COMMUNITIES OF INTEREST AND VALUE MIGRATION

Staying on top of demographic trends has always been challenging, but today the effort of keeping up can be truly overwhelming. And it's now possible to differentiate interest groups in ways that were never possible before, using data capable of pinpointing even the tiniest market segment. Communities of interest might include patients with HIV, single working moms, aging Baby Boomers, high-net-worth individuals, and HDTV aficionados; they may reside in the United States, Thailand, or Egypt. These communities are not only more numerous (in terms of possible slices of the market) than traditional demographic groups—they're more powerful. They communicate across all borders via the Internet, and they share information about products, services, and companies within their spheres. Word of a problem with a new product spreads instantly, as does word of an emerging, must-have innovation. And none of these groups have to rely on visiting brick-and-mortar establishments to get what they need—they can order online from anywhere in the world. On top of all this, communities of interest are impacted by a growing, worldwide community of regulators. When one regulatory group on one side of the world denies approval for a new product, it's likely that another regulatory body, aware of this denial, will follow suit.

Companies cannot win in diverse markets unless they know what business they are in, who they serve, and how they create value. Global organizations must differentiate, but from a consistently integrated global brand. At the same time, they need to follow the customer as the value proposition keeps evolving.

To develop a better sense of the impact of value migration on organizations, consider the following sequence. A community of interest decides it wants not only a high-quality product but better prices. At the same time suppliers (some from foreign countries with different business models) begin to compete with high-quality products by offering the same (or similar) products at lower prices, precipitating a value migration. This forces all suppliers to reorganize their production systems or find other ways to lower costs. If this community of interest then decides it wants this product faster, production and delivery systems must be reorganized yet again to achieve higher efficiencies. As an organization attempts to win in more and more diverse markets, it must confront an ever-increasing number of value propositions based on varied buying preferences, cultural differences, and regulatory conditions. The diversity of global markets with a range of values creates complexity of demand. As a result, this demand not only drives value migration but challenges all suppliers to determine whether they will go to market on one differentiator or try to compete on all new values simultaneously—in all markets. Each company has to decide if it will compete on quality, price, or speed—or all three—and whether the value proposition should be the same in all markets.

Here is the perfect storm challenge to leaders: managing constant organizational change to sell different products in different ways to different communities of interest in different countries, while keeping costs down and guaranteeing a consistent brand experience.

Consider the changes taking place in the hotel industry. Once-single-branded hotels now have multiple brands that cater to different customers. Hilton has five full-service brands—Doubletree, Embassy Suites, Hilton, Hilton Garden Inn, and Homewood Suites. Yet all must ensure a consistent experience for Hilton customers. Hotels must set global brand consistency while acknowledging the importance of local culture, particularly as hotel chains expand globally. At the same time the expectations of leisure and business customers are changing. Both are no longer interested in just a place to sleep, but also a place to live, whether this means broadband access over the Internet or twenty-four-hour fitness centers. This has had a significant impact on the design and amenities required to satisfy customers.

Just about every industry is facing similar conundrums involving its communities of interest. For this reason, companies must understand their customers at a deeper level than has ever been required before. Nokia's quest to add 2 billion customers in the next few years—especially customers in markets such as India and China—reflects the significance of this challenge. Nokia designed a mobile phone for emerging market customers that relied on anthropological research to help leaders get into the mind-set of this particular community of interest. In doing so it discovered that one of its assumptions about cell phone users was wrong: One phone was often not used by just one customer. Instead, phones were shared among members of villages or families because of the relatively high costs of the phones. The company created a different type of cell phone, one that was more rugged (because a shared phone requires durability), included a shared address book feature, a call tracker device that limits time and cost per call, and a one-touch flashlight that facilitates usage during the power outages common to these areas. None of these features would have been included if Nokia had failed to undertake the research on customer needs in emerging markets.

The Dangers of Being Too Differentiated

We've said before that the secret to success in leveraging diversity is to find the right balance between integration and differentiation. Everyone wants to win in diverse, developing markets, but not everyone is aware of the costs. In pursuit of victory globally, companies can move with speed and purpose—and end up winning battles while losing the war. Pursuing a diversity-based strategy globally is a tricky business. Hidden pitfalls abound, and what makes perfect sense on paper may not turn out well in the real world. We've found that many leaders embark on global market strategies with great expectations and end up being blindsided. Here are four common mistakes:

Tarnishing the brand or losing focus for the sake of winning everywhere.

You take an Alexander the Great stance—when you want to conquer the world, no customer is too small, no market too insignificant. But when you attempt to win in too many diverse markets, you may find yourself diluting your brand or spreading your resources too thin. Citigroup has a presence in over 125 countries around the world and is considered one of the strongest global franchises in financial services. But its presence in some markets is very small and some have criticized it for lack of focus on those markets where it could have achieved scale and greater returns on the investment.

Nike is a company that is constantly pushing the innovation envelope to create products to give the world's greatest athletes a competitive advantage. Athletes are its most demanding consumer. The development of Nike+, the social networking system that gives runners a motivational tool to run with music, is just the latest chapter of how the company creates new consumer experiences and connections, making customers better athletes.

Several years ago Nike executives noticed people all over the world running with music. Nike approached Apple with the idea to combine music and sport. The result? The Nike+iPod experience. It's a simple system built around a Nike+ iPod sport kit, which includes a sensor that can be placed in a Nike+ enabled running shoe to talk to the chip placed in the runner's iPod Nano. The resulting data, which include pace, distance, and calories burned, are sent to Nike, via www.nikeplus.com, which in turn can provide training tips based on the data received. The technology has been extremely successful: more than 1.2 million members signed up at last count. Nike Plus has since become the world's largest running club and the gold standard for fitness training. Nike has been leveraging the success of the Nike Plus online community to create new running events, such as the Nike+ Human Race last August, which brought together twenty-five cities around the world to celebrate their love of running, in what the company billed as, the "world's largest 10K race."

Nike Plus is a great product that could provide many ways to expand to diverse groups around the world, but Nike is keenly aware of the importance of targeting the right consumer. Nike as a brand represents very specific, authentic qualities—fitness, training, athleticism—and if the community is to continue growing, it must keep its communications youthful. That is why it recently introduced avatars and iPhone applications to keep those connections strong.

Always trying to create better mousetraps.

This is the traditional mind-set of innovative companies. They assume that if they create a great product, they will possess the power to dictate the terms of its purchase. They decide what customers want and need, the pace at which they will receive it, and where they can buy it. Market leaders especially tend to view diverse markets as if they, rather than the customer, are in charge. But markets are no longer static, especially the communities of interest that are plugged into the Internet and know of new developments at the same time as, or even before, business leaders. Customers move with astonishing speed these days, and what was a better mousetrap can become a worse one overnight. Companies that choose to compete in diverse markets also face the challenges of meeting competition from the very markets they are trying to enter.

Being overly responsive to perceived needs of the customer.

It's not just mousetrap building that gets companies in trouble; slavishly following the perceived needs of the customer can also prove a pitfall. Obviously, companies must try and shape the market when opportunities arise and create demand through new, interesting, or exciting products. Doing so based only on what customers tell you they want, however, can be a doomed strategy. Customers often don't know what they want until they see it, and companies that relentlessly pursue and ask for customer insights often end up with incremental innovation. A well-known business magazine was almost run into the ground some years ago by a brilliant editor who relied entirely on data and fact from focus groups and customer research to make decisions, producing a product that lacked creativity and a unique point of view—a product readers did not like, even though they had asked for it.

Sometimes customers will lie when you ask them a question. For example, some *People* magazine readers won't acknowledge reading the publication because they don't want to be seen as being interested in celebrities and pop culture. Voting research has long proven the same fact. In market research, asking customers is important, but insufficient for breakthrough innovation.

Failing to question your assumptions.

Many companies fall into the trap of pursuing strategies based on assumptions that are no longer true. We've watched leaders inadvertently let momentum, past success, or hope cloud their judgment when it comes to meeting customer needs in particular markets.

One company that seems to have done an excellent job of questioning assumptions is Procter & Gamble. P&G, like most companies that entered China earlier in the decade or even before that, focused on the country's large cities. It assumed that reaching rural customers—scattered over a huge geographical area and with much less money and buying sophistication than city dwellers—would be much tougher. To its credit, P&G soon began questioning this assumption. It analyzed Chinese markets and recognized that it was facing competition in the cities so intense that it was invariably going to diminish sales volume and profitability. After careful consideration, it began shifting the strategy to the countryside.

This wasn't merely a conceptual shift but one that required reorganizing the whole distribution system to establish sufficient outlets in rural areas. Its brand managers also recognized that rural Chinese had requirements and aspirations different from those who lived in cities. Instead of selling Morning Lotus Fragrance Crest Toothpaste for $1 in the cities, P&G sold Crest Salt White for 50 cents (based on the widespread rural belief that salt whitens teeth). Today, the majority of P&G's Chinese customers live outside the twenty-four largest cities.

P&G is not alone among Western companies scrambling to reach the Chinese consumer in new ways. Johnson & Johnson makes a number of global products for babies and parents. It also has a very successful U.S. Internet site called BabyCenter.com. J&J recognizes that the number of parents, especially mothers, on the Internet in China today is significant in both rural and urban areas—and so it is questioning its traditional retail approaches to develop interactive communication with Chinese consumers. In Chinese homes throughout the country, consumers have access to television and soon will have the Internet as well. J&J recognizes the need to leapfrog the technology and reach Chinese consumers where they will be in the future, not just today.

If you want to win in diverse markets, you need to take numerous and untraditional factors into consideration. You can't just think about meeting customer needs. You also need to keep tabs on suppliers and potential problems that might arise—if a supplier has trouble delivering your product because its competition has outmaneuvered it, you're the one who will suffer. You need to understand exactly how you make money from a customer relationship, and recognize that the way you create and deliver products may no longer be effective in a diverse marketplace—what worked when your markets were relatively homogeneous probably doesn't work as well today.

The pharmaceutical industry is slowly coming to terms with this reality. Its traditional time-consuming, science-driven process can result in an excellent product for which no profitable market exists when it's finally ready. Wyeth CEO Robert Essner has observed that companies in his industry used to assume that if they did great science, good products would emerge from it. Wyeth, he said, has been trying to "find the middle ground between great science and rigorous process . . . reducing cost and improving efficiency on the development side and constantly improving the quality of science on the discovery side." For all pharmaceuticals, the emerging business model is unclear. Can ten-year investments in discovery for new compounds that may or may not achieve regulatory approval continue in a cost-constrained health care environment?

WHOLE LEADERSHIP APPROACH TO DIVERSE MARKETS: DIFFERENTIATE AND INTEGRATE

Partial leaders used to be able to win in diverse markets. They practiced the equivalent of corporate imperialism, invading new countries and dictating terms. They showed little heart and less guts, but plenty of analytical muscle—charting growth curves that matched product introductions in other countries.

Now, not only are different head qualities required, but without real empathy and astute intuition, companies will lose. In fact, those companies that set out to "change China" or "change India" may be in big trouble. The degree of influence emerging markets will exert on large, complex global companies will be significant. They will become more "Chinese" or more "Indian" than they realize, if they are to compete and grow. How can head, heart, and guts help organizations do well in a great diversity of markets? Consider the factors outlined in Figure 6.1.

1. *Use your head to track customer value migration on a global scale.*

The cognitive skills required to do well in various global markets have changed. It used to be a purely analytical game, focused mostly on tracking satisfaction data from traditional customers, that anyone could play. Then it became a matter of understanding new

FIGURE 6.1. *Differentiate and Integrate Your Markets.*

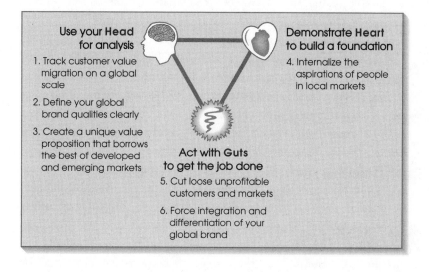

customers—customers who often had different requirements from traditional customers. Today, it's being able to reinvent the company continuously, based on value migration. Knowing how and when to change your business design to meet an ever-changing value stream demands keen perception, an innovative mind-set, and a relentless focus on current and future markets. This requires enormous flexibility—around costs, decision-making, and swift transfer of best practices from one market to another to stay competitive. It means fewer silos and more outward focus on what is actually happening in the market, on the ground.

2. *Use your head to define your global brand qualities clearly.*

Necessary as it is to understand what customers value and how this varies from country to country and market to market, leaders must also determine how they go to market from a brand perspective. In a complex, information-rich marketplace, brand becomes even more important to differentiate among the disorder and build an ongoing relationship with the consumer. The challenge is knowing what elements of your brand proposition can be integrated and what can be differentiated without risk. In other words, determine how the brand can be defined globally but differentiated locally.

Many companies struggle with this paradox, with global franchise teams defining and mandating characteristics only to have local marketing teams say, "Wait! In our market, that won't work!" Managing this paradox impacts your approach to product innovation, packaging, and supply chain, and your choice of marketing and advertising firms. It also requires defining clear roles and developing constructive ways to manage conflict. Sometimes it requires elevating decisions, especially around brand, to higher levels and expanding beyond just the marketing perspective.

3. *Use your head to create a unique value proposition that borrows the best of developed and emerging markets.*

In a global world, value quickly moves around, especially knowledge of product offerings, features, and benefits not available but easily seen on the Internet. Leaders entering emerging markets must adapt quickly to the definition of value, whether it is price, quality, quantity, packaging, or other features. Blending developed market quality with emerging market price expectations is a challenge for many leaders today, but getting it right is key to competing effectively. While China has produced low-cost/high-value offerings in clothing, home decorating, and other low-end products for Wal-Mart and other retailers, we are witnessing value migrating to the high end, with unique offerings developed for markets such as India or China in more sophisticated industries such as medical devices, electronics, computers, and even cars soon to be available in developed markets at lower prices, where they will probably do well.

4. *Use your heart to internalize the aspirations of people in local markets.*

As nice as it would be to succeed in diverse markets through analysis alone, it can't be done anymore. It takes the ability to identify with the dreams of people in Brazil, the hopes of individuals in Russia. Ask these questions: What does a man living in the Chinese countryside think of an iPod? Where does that fit into his lifestyle? What does this product mean in terms of how he sees himself, the type of music that is meaningful to him? Would a Chinese woman answer these questions differently? What about someone who lives in Sichuan compared to someone in Hunan province? The questions are numerous, and the answers can only be found if you possess a sense of who people really are and what drives them. You can't develop this intuition sitting in a corporate office thousands of miles away and reading consumer data.

We run leadership programs for many Western executives in developing countries. Frequently we immerse leaders in the market. We take them to an orphanage in India to help bathe, feed, and play with children; to Chinese homes in the countryside to sit down at the kitchen table and discuss hopes, concerns, and needs. No matter how great the cultural divide, these executives are always surprised by how universal human aspirations can be, and how cultural differences can impact almost everything. Being in the market, living there, relating to people opens up the heart and also develops real market and customer intuition.

5. *Use your guts to cut loose unprofitable customers and markets.*

Winning companies and leaders identify who their most profitable customers and markets are and will be. This begins as a head competency, with facts that define market, product, and profit growth potential. This may seem obvious, but many companies lack the inclination or capacity to differentiate and fully understand how they're making money or how much a customer costs. Even when they obtain this data, they have difficulty acting on it. It takes real guts to jettison customers and markets that either cost too much or don't provide the revenue they once did, in order to free up cash for other investments.

Contrary to what you might think, extensive analysis often doesn't provide the motivation to act. This inaction is especially prevalent in professional service firms, whose senior partners develop close relationships with clients over a long period of time. When the firm's managing partner decides that these clients have to go, senior partners are often infuriated—and threatened with the loss of client income—even though the connection may no longer be profitable for the firm. And the same is true of sales reps, marketing directors, or country managers whose personal loyalty to a product or customer makes it difficult to cut the cord.

6. *Use your guts to force integration and differentiation of your global brand.*

Leaders need to make some tough choices—and they need to explain these choices to clients and customers with heart—openly and honestly. If they don't, they'll miss opportunities in all types of markets. The decision to end a customer relationship is more difficult if it's profitable today, but declining. It takes guts to do something different in the face of current success. We work with many global companies that have developed a portfolio of brands and come to love the brands almost like children.

When it becomes clear that some of the brands have limited future potential without significant investment, leaders struggle to act because of their real affection for the brand.

But this is often the only way to marshal the resources to accelerate the growth of other brands, or enter a new market. Many companies want to focus on developing markets but need to cut back on serving customers in Western markets so as to shift resources. It's difficult—and it requires astute prioritization and reorganization, and sometimes the obvious but difficult action needs to be taken. As problematic as this is to do, if leaders do it properly, the decision will likely pay off in the long run.

Leaders tend to follow what they see as tried-and-true global strategies—strategies that may be tried, but are no longer true. They are tempted to follow a successful formula because their head tells them it makes sense, failing to heed what their intuition tells them may be the need for another direction or unwilling to make a bold decision about a market that feels foreign in more than one sense.

WHOLE LEADERSHIP QUESTIONS TO ASK YOURSELF ABOUT DIFFERENTIATING AND INTEGRATING MARKET DIVERSITY

Questioning assumptions helps you assess whether you're lapsing into partial leadership. By continuously assessing whether you're approaching diverse markets at full capacity, you stand a better chance of winning. Therefore, consider these head, heart, and guts market questions:

Use Your Head
- Who are your customers?
- Where should you be serving them?
- What does value look like in your customers' minds? What are they willing to pay for?
- How is the value going to shift? How long will your current business design work?
- How do you create value?
- How profitable are your customers? How much is one customer relationship worth compared to another?
- What might you have to do in terms of reorganizing manufacturing, distribution, and so on as value migration occurs in different markets?

Use Your Heart

- Do you understand and respond to your customers' hopes and dreams?
- Do you sense what drives your customers—their likes and dislikes, concerns and goals?
- Are you able to relate to different customers in different markets? Can you differentiate your customers' needs?
- Do you make an effort to get to know the communities of interest and other customer groups with which you're unfamiliar?
- Do you spend significant time on Web sites and in other countries developing relationships with your customers?
- Are you willing and able to make decisions based on hunches and instinct as well as on data and fact?
- Have you created a customer-centric culture? Do your people understand and care about your customers as much as you do?

Use Your Guts

- Are you willing to tell a long-time customer the relationship is no longer working?
- Are you willing to move away from a profitable customer that you believe will not be profitable (or as profitable) in the future?
- Do you make decisions about the "customer of tomorrow"? Do you take risks on megafactors (such as changes in the price of oil) that will impact your future mix of customers?
- Are you able to pull out of a market where you've made a significant investment to go into a new market that offers the possibility of a greater return?
- Can you make the right trade-offs when it comes to striking a balance between differentiation and integration?

We understand that no one can answer yes to all these questions all the time. A perfect storm makes every leader imperfect, and diversity compounded by uncertainty and complexity sometimes causes action to come from the head when it should come from the heart or the guts. Whole leaders, though, make the effort to ask these questions continuously, developing their whole leader consciousness. In this way, they're aware of the three distinct capabilities that are necessary for succeeding in diverse markets.

CHAPTER

7

Learn to Lead Everyone

U NDERSTANDING HUMAN MOTIVATION IS AT THE CORE OF
successful leadership. Many of us grew up with Western theories
that proclaimed that everyone on earth was motivated by three, four,
or five basic needs. Today, our understanding of human motivation
is much more complex. Lawrence and Nohria offer a contemporary
view of motivation based on their research. They found that people
are driven by four needs:

- *To acquire:* The need to obtain everything from goods and services
  to status and rewards in order to achieve a sense of well-being.
- *To bond:* The need for a sense of belonging through groups, organizations, and associations.
- *To comprehend:* The need to make sense of the world and to learn
  and grow from experience.
- *To defend:* The need for security and prevention from harm.

While it may be true that everyone in the world has the same
basic needs, the intensity of these needs will vary from person to person. Equally important, the way these needs are expressed and met
varies widely from one society to another and from one generation
to another. It would be nice to be able to grasp this range of needs
quickly and accurately, but perceptions become clouded during periods of great change, when struggling with major business dilemmas,
or grappling with other turbulent issues.

Learning to lead *everyone* requires a full range of leadership capacities: deep empathy, a broad understanding of the diversity of values, beliefs, and motives that drive human behavior, and the willingness to make tough choices in the face of these differences. Motivational theories may provide clues, but learning how people express and get their needs met around the world is one of the keys to leadership today.

BEYOND DIVERSITY

This isn't about diversity for diversity's sake. It's not about liberal guilt or sitting around just trying to understand each other. It's not about doing the right thing and creating a better world—though these are admirable goals. It's not even about achieving consensus. *It's about understanding and leveraging diversity of cultures and generations for competitive advantage.*

As we noted in Chapter Two, *diversity* is an emotionally charged, overused term, and it can cause organizations to create training programs that are highly moralistic . . . but not highly pertinent to the purpose of the organization. It can also make employees all too aware of their differences, increasing tension among various groups. But even more important, as noted earlier, traditional diversity programs and training don't work.

When companies launch major diversity training initiatives, it suggests that they're trying to prove to themselves that they believe everyone is equal. In fact, a recent study revealed that diversity training is inversely proportional to the level of diversity in an organization. It's fine to teach people to be tolerant of other groups, but this type of training generally only touches the surface layer of bias.

Mahzarin Banaji's study of unconscious bias suggests that everyone operates with unacknowledged prejudice that has a multiple impact within organizations. For example, these biases may predispose a manager to give John a big raise and Joan a small one or, more subtly, to listen more closely to what John has to say than to Joan's comments—or vice versa.

You can't simply talk people out of their biases. If you try to tell them about unconscious bias (or discuss hiring a coach to work with them as individuals), they'll look at you like you're crazy. People truly believe themselves to be no more biased than anyone else.

So what is a leader to do? People who are resolutely cognitive in their approach tend to favor diversity training programs as the logical response to a diversity problem. Whole leaders, on the other hand, use their heads to help others understand what unconscious biases are all about and which ones impact their behavior, they display the guts to confront these biases and prompt the type of discussions that raise everyone's awareness of the problems these biases cause, and they display the heart to appreciate how the bias originated and try to understand the logic behind it.

None of these approaches solves the problem. But they create an environment where unconscious bias is brought out in the open and can be managed, doing far less damage than it otherwise would.

Learning to lead everyone isn't easy at the best of times, and it's even more difficult when a new crisis seems to strike every day and the complexities of dealing with the resulting problems are overwhelming. Partial leaders may make a valiant effort to consider different people and points of view, but under the stress of a perfect storm, they lose focus on the need to lead everyone. Whole leaders take a different approach, and one of the best ways to see how this approach plays out is by examining the often subtle but significant cultural differences that impact all global companies.

LEVERAGING NATIONAL CULTURAL IDENTITY

"Who are you?" has different answers in different cultures. It may seem obvious that how you lead depends on who you lead, but in reality most leaders tend to impose their leadership philosophy on everyone, regardless of age, gender, or country of origin. They tend to forget that behavior varies considerably among different groups, and this is especially true when dealing with employees in foreign countries. This is due in some part to the fact that global organizations today sincerely want all employees to think of themselves as one brand—as McDonald's, IBM, or Federal Express—rather than as, say, Spanish employees working for McDonald's.

Behaviorally, however, people respond very differently to organizational programs and policies, even though they may identify with the organization as a whole. At Nike, attracting and keeping top talent is a major issue in its Chinese company. To attract and keep top talent in America, Nike does what most smart organizations do: demonstrate the career benefits of being at Nike and provide employees with rewards and personally challenging career paths. In China, though, whether an employee joins or stays with a company is many times a family issue. The decision to join an organization is made by the family, not the individual. Nike's talent strategy in China depends on recognizing the importance of family in the Chinese culture and how family impacts career.

Earley and Mosakowski have underscored the need for leaders to learn to cope with different national and corporate cultures based on their Cultural Intelligence (CQ): the ability to make sense of unfamiliar contexts and then blend in. They describe three components to CQ—the cognitive, the physical, and the emotional/motivational. In surveys of two thousand leaders in sixty countries they found that few are equally strong in all three of these areas. They argue that CQ is an important factor in determining the success of leaders of global companies.

Whole leadership requires thinking about cultural differences from a broad perspective. To facilitate this type of wide-ranging thought, consider these two key questions:

- Is the culture group-oriented or individualistic?
- Is the culture hierarchical or egalitarian?

Is the culture group-oriented or individualistic? In group-oriented cultures, people identify themselves in terms of family, tribe, caste, ethnicity, or religion. In Nigeria, someone you ask "Who are you?" may respond with a tribal identification first: "I'm an Ebo." In the United States, a highly individualistic culture, people respond to that question with their name. In many Asian societies, a person's family name comes first and individual identification second. In such societies, the criteria for decision making are reversed. The first concern is what others may think or want—or how to maintain harmony in the group—be it family, tribe, or clan. As a result, others beyond the employee are involved in making decisions about how to act in all aspects of life. Witness Nike working to involve the family in work decisions.

This can lead to challenging problems. Many group-oriented societies do not differentiate between what is expected in a person's behavior in the local family or tribe and what is expected at work. For example, in many family and clan societies it is expected that everyone will take care of everyone else. This provides an excellent social network for day-to-day life. But when family and clan members expect their family member, having gained a position of authority and responsibility as a local employee of a Western company, to give jobs to other family or clan members, there can be a difficult clash between local social values and global business values—and the local employee is caught in the middle. It is very hard to explain to your relatives that you cannot fulfill what they see as a primary family obligation.

Is the culture hierarchical or egalitarian? Group-oriented countries tend to be hierarchical. In China, for example, the hierarchical system can be traced back to Confucianism, which prescribed behavior between dynasties and subjects, parents and children, older and younger siblings, and in many other social relationships. In these hierarchical societies, people have certain responsibilities and obligations based on where they are in the societal order. More specifically, the lower down you are in the hierarchy, the less able you are to voice your opinion to someone above you. Peasants don't tell kings that they don't approve of the new tax on chickens. In Thailand, you can ask Thais working in a factory what's wrong with the production line, and they may all know full well that the feeder system isn't functioning properly. But none of them will tell you. They believe it's not their place to point out a flaw in the system. As the leader, you may be perceived as the person of higher authority—you should know—and it would be disrespectful to presume to tell you something you should know.

In the same way, when global companies send out employee surveys in these societies and are delighted to find that everyone seems happy and satisfied, they don't realize that people in hierarchical societies don't grasp the concept of filling out the survey with complete honesty. In an egalitarian society such as the United States, of course, people are more than happy to share their complaints.

Beyond understanding that group-oriented and individualistic societies may make decisions differently and that hierarchy plays a much more important role in management and supervisory relations in some cultures than in others, global leaders today also face seemingly irreconcilable value choices when doing business in other countries. What a U.S. leader views as ethical and acceptable business practices often runs into a wall of unacceptable values and beliefs in another society.

In China, a deeply ingrained system of reciprocity exists: if someone does something for you, you're obligated to do something for that person. In India, a variation on this theme exists. People who have collected the most "chits" possess the most power—their capacity to call in these chits when they need assistance is compelling. In Russia, they have *Blat,* a term that refers to an informal system of clout through connections, nepotism, and bribes. That means that companies wanting to do business there may have to hire someone who has pull with the government rather than the candidate best qualified for a job. Or these companies may need to hire the son of a powerful politician to arrange a deal that is critical for their operation. These moves may fly in the face of a company's stated values.

Global leaders are caught between moral absolutism (clear right-versus-wrong business decisions) and cultural relativism (figuring out what's needed to operate effectively in a given country and then trying to be as ethical as possible within those limits). When you stringently enforce a code of corporate values (beyond issues of legal compliance), you may provide clarity to your employees regarding their expected behavior in your corporate culture, but you may be distancing them from their customers and giving their competitors an advantage. On the other hand, if you "go with the local culture" in trying to be responsive and sensitive to local needs, you may have such a diversity of policies and practices around the world that your company has no brand and your people are confused about what you and the company stand for. This tension has no easy answers, but whole leaders are able to engage their heart to understand cultural differences, their head to analyze the impact of these differences on the business, and their guts to determine what values they want their companies to stand for.

At the same time, you don't have to make things more difficult than they already are. Many of us who were raised in rational, cognitive systems try to apply logic to doing business in foreign countries—logic that fails to function in what we see as illogical environments. But it's not just a matter of empathy. It is also absolutely essential that whole leaders develop their own belief system independent of traditional organizational beliefs. This is what allows them to deal with the maddening ethical dilemmas of doing business in places like China and Russia. When they know what they believe, they have a foundation for taking risks—for deciding it's okay to walk a fine line between what's right in the United States and what's right in another country—but only if they have well-defined limits based on their own values and beliefs.

Finally, consider the need for whole leadership in a country like India. Imagine you work for IBM, which has hired fifty-three thousand people and is the country's largest foreign employer. Or Google. Or Yahoo. Your local employees include Muslims, Hindus, Sikhs, and Buddhists. They are members of different castes. They speak twenty-two different languages. Leading in this diverse culture is impossible if you're one-dimensional. If you can't relate to people with a wide range of religious and social beliefs, you're going to struggle. If you don't come across as someone with a clear vision about the business, you're going to find yourself unable to take necessary risks. The challenges, as well as the opportunities, in countries such as India can't be overstated. To meet the former and capitalize on the latter, whole leadership is crucial. And many partial leaders—overrelying on head, heart, or guts (usually head)—have failed abroad after many successful years in their domestic operations.

LEVERAGING DIFFERENCES IN THE SEARCH FOR MEANING

The differences are not just cross-cultural. They exist within each society and among different subgroups. Leaders used to have it a lot easier in terms of satisfying the requirements of their people. For the most part, employees shared common expectations of what an employer would give them—expectations that revolved around compensation and included employee loyalty and employer security. But now a diverse domestic workforce wants different things from an organization. Age, gender, sexual orientation, personal philosophy, and many other factors influence what people want, and it's not only about money. In fact, in recent years we've observed the appearance of something we call "the money-meaning gap," and it's a gap that's growing.

The Money-Meaning Gap

The *money-meaning gap* is the divide between an organization's emphasis on profit and all the factors that make work a purposeful, values-based endeavor for employees. Though compensation remains a significant aspect of what most individuals get out of a work experience, it is no longer the only thing or even the major thing. In many Asian countries there are those who simply expect to be given challenging assignments where they are learning and growing constantly. And in any large organization, you'll find a percentage of employees who want to work for a company that is environmentally conscious or contributes to making the world a better place in some other way. Or you'll find a significant number of people who want to work for companies where their particular minority is treated fairly. And still others might want to be part of an organization that offers them freedom in terms of where and when they work. Sometimes these differences are expressed in generational terms, such as "Boomers" versus "Millennials." These represent generalizations, usually valid in some way, about what people want and expect from their work.

Each generation shares a common set of characteristics that differentiate its members, to some degree, from other generations:

- Traditionalists—used to homogeneous families and neighbors; shaped by post-WWII world and growth in white-collar jobs
- Boomers—children of causes and revolution; shaped by the Vietnam War and the Civil Rights movement
- Gen Xers—accustomed to a diverse group of friends; shaped by the end of the Cold War, women in workforce, and growth of the Internet
- Millennials or Gen Yers—raised to be upbeat and determined; shaped by routine terrorism, bull market, ubiquitous technology and collaboration reflected in online communities.

Being responsive to these different motivations while continuing to meet ever more challenging financial requirements vexes many leaders. How much time and effort can you put into training and development programs or "good works" when demands for performance from Wall Street drive short-term decisions? At the same time, leaders ignore these nonfinancial values at their peril. Imagine being the CEO of a company that a national magazine designates as "one of the worst places for women to work" or is attacked in the media for its massive carbon footprint or other neglect of the environment.

The best leaders can identify with the values and desires of various employee segments and their widely varying definitions of meaningful work (and workplaces). They recognize the need to invest time and money in programs that close the money-meaning gap. And they understand that if they do not pay attention to these differing concerns, they will pay a price in terms of employee retention or corporate reputation.

Each has a different set of expectations of you as a leader. Table 7.1 summarizes some of the major differences.

Consider just a few of the ways the so-called Millennial Generation define what's meaningful to them:

Millennials (people born between 1977 and 2000), like all generations, possess certain attitudes and beliefs that stem from their upbringing. Unlike older workers, they were raised in high-tech settings, and the dangers of pollution, global warming, and other ecological disasters surrounded them. They were exposed to violent incidents in cities, including the attacks on 9/11, and in schools—such

TABLE 7.1. *Generations at Work.*

Generation	Traditionalist	Boomer	GenXer	Millennial/GenYer
Leadership	Hierarchy	Consensus	Competence	Pulling together
Feedback	No news is good news	Once a year with documentation	ATM— Interrupts and asks how they are doing	"Gamer Generation"— touch of a button; 500 X
Work Ethic	Work hard; save money; what is play?	Work hard; play hard; worry about money	Work hard, if it doesn't interfere with play; save money	Work hard as one of multiple priorities—family and the planet; save money
Balance	Don't quite get it	Sandwich generation	Want balance now	Need flexibility to create it

Source: Human Resources Institute, St. Petersburg, Florida, 2007.

as Columbine and Virginia Tech. Their parents impressed upon them the need for safety (from bike helmets to Halloween candy dos and don'ts) and encouraged them to have a sense of self and self-esteem.

Leaders need to be sensitive to new concerns Millennials bring with them. We see these concerns expressed in employee meetings, on surveys, and on chat boards. "What is our company doing to be Green?" they ask. "Why don't people have options to work at home, at night, and on weekends? Why don't we have a 'Corporate Facebook' so I can find colleagues working on similar projects? Why don't we have a more open, casual environment where people can network and collaborate? Do we have [X] state-of-the-art computer technology?"

Millennials are the most networked and collaborative generation ever. Having grown up with Facebook and Instant Messaging, they expect to be able to work in teams and with others on tasks they consider meaningful and important. They expect continuous, ongoing feedback about their performance, as though they were playing a computer game; an annual performance appraisal seems far too remote. Managing these expectations will take all the head, heart, and guts leaders can muster.

Employees need belonging and connection.

Not only the Millennials but people in general are experiencing a greater need for belonging, especially at a time when some may no longer belong to organized religion or social or volunteer clubs, or may move frequently from one location to another, as the rate of divorce approaches 50 percent. These individuals expect their organizations to provide a sense of inclusion. This can mean everything from flourishing online communities to participatory decision making. Inclusion and connection, at least to a certain extent, are matters of perception.

As the disparity between the highest-paid and lowest-paid members of organizations grows, people perceive top executives as haves and themselves as have-nots. If the rank and file view senior managers as arrogant or isolated, cynicism develops and employees become less committed and loyal. Leaders can foster a sense of inclusion in a thousand different ways—making their presence felt by walking and talking around the office, creating knowledge exchanges that solicit and use employee ideas. However, if you can't relate to this need for inclusion, you won't respond to it.

Team members desire a sense of impact.

When organizations were more hierarchical and clear top-to-bottom reporting existed, employees saw how their work translated directly into the implementation of strategies and achievement of goals. In today's matrix structures, by contrast, multiple teams work on the same projects, people report to more than one manager, and it's often difficult to know how much of an impact they had on the finished product. Many team members have felt as if they were working in a vacuum, tossing months of hard work into a project and never hearing a sound in response. They crave feedback. Leaders need to create systems where team members are recognized for their individual as well as team contributions. They need to communicate to people how their work on a given team helped achieve both short-term and long-term objectives.

Satisfying these diverse constituencies is daunting because they are more informed than previous generations of employees. The Internet has raised their awareness of what other companies are doing for their people (or for the environment or other good causes) and where their own company falls short. Employee chat boards allow them to exchange information with colleagues, giving them an outlet to complain and ratchet up their indignation. As a result, organizational leaders can't ignore dissatisfied employee groups and hope the upset will pass. It won't pass; information technology feeds and sustains it.

LEARNING TO LEAD EVERYONE FOR COMPETITIVE ADVANTAGE

It is becoming increasingly clear that organizations that can leverage a wide range of diverse perspectives will have a better chance of competing in a global world. Diverse employees, from different social, cultural, racial, ethnic, and gender backgrounds, can ensure that companies have thought through the product and policy consequences of their decisions to have maximum competitive advantage.

At the same time, a great deal of research has shown that if organizations cannot manage these differences successfully, having diversity in an organization provides no significant advantage.

Managing everyone for a competitive advantage means that everyone must be heard. This in turn brings us back to whole leadership.

Partial leaders many times fail to include diverse opinions and fail to reconcile differences when they appear. Head leaders may dominate conversations as the "smartest person in the room." Heart leaders may be open to a wide range of opinions without being able to resolve the differences when they are expressed. And in some instances sensitivity to cultural differences and a desire not to have anyone be embarrassed may lead some people to avoid bringing out different opinions in order to avoid conflict and embarrassment.

Whole leadership allows diversity to be heard, to be confronted, and to be reconciled. At the very least, it makes it possible for decisions to be made and action taken.

WHOLE LEADERSHIP AND LEARNING TO LEAD EVERYONE

Developing leaders to both understand diversity and use it to maximum advantage requires the steps shown in Figure 7.1.

FIGURE 7.1. *Learn to Lead Everyone.*

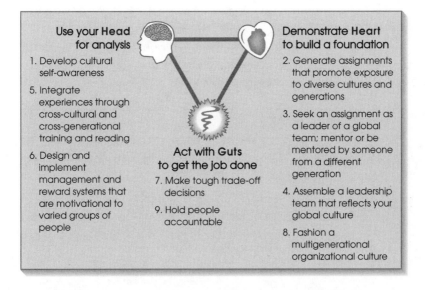

1. *Use your head to develop cultural self-awareness.*

People need a way to discover their own biases and find out how perceptive they are about differences between groups. Administering a new instrument such as the TMA's Country Navigator (sketched in Table 7.2) or the TMC's Cultural Orientation Indicator provides experiences or feedback that develops cultural self-awareness: understanding of what it means to be from your particular culture and how you may be different from people who have been raised in other cultures.

2. *Use your heart to generate assignments that promote exposure to diverse cultures and generations.*

For leaders, taking on assignments or projects abroad is usually an eye-opening and consciousness-raising experience. It is astonishing that in this global age, many executives have never spent a significant amount of time—at least four weeks—working in another country. When they do, a colleague from that country's office will invariably say something like, "You Americans always act this way when . . ." For the first time, they can look at themselves from the outside in. Americans, for example, may begin to understand what it means to be brought up in an individualistic society if they spend time in countries like Korea and Japan, which are obviously more group oriented and also more hierarchical. At the very least, it will start them thinking about their cultural values and how they differ from those of others.

3. *Use your heart to seek an assignment as a leader of a global team; mentor or be mentored by someone from a different generation.*

Leaders need to be assigned to global teams. This gives them the opportunity of learning about diversity on the job. To succeed on a global team, they need to figure out their own way of working with

---

TABLE 7.2. *The TMA Worldprism™: Cultural Orientation.*

RELATING (How we interact)	Focus: Task—Relationship
	Communication: Explicit—Implicit
	Identity: Individual—Group
REGULATING (How we manage)	Behavior: Risk Taking—Risk Avoiding
	Use of Time: Tight—Loose
	Power: Shared—Concentrated
REASONING (How we think)	Processing: Linear—Circular
	Emphasis: Facts—Thinking
	Explanation: Simple—Complex

other people who have very different backgrounds, business philosophies, and behaviors. Many companies today conduct launch workshops when global teams are convened, sessions in which the team not only defines its purpose, roles, responsibilities, and action plan but also explores cultural differences and how they might affect the team's work together.

From a generational perspective, it is important to find ways to understand the values and perspectives of both older and younger employees. In one of Jack Welch's famous moves as CEO of General Electric, he required every one of his top 250 senior executives to be mentored in technology by someone under thirty at least a few hours each month. His hidden agenda was that in addition to learning something about technology, his senior executives would also learn something about the perspectives and needs of the younger generation in GE.

4. *Use your heart to assemble a leadership team that reflects your global culture.*

Make sure that your leadership team looks like the mix of cultures you're leading. Too often executive teams are homogeneous. At Siemens, for example, all but one member of the top team is German. Contrast that with Vodafone where ten nationalities are represented among the top twenty-two executives. As CEO Arun Sarin says, "We have a group of executives here that is far more diverse at the absolute senior level than any company I know. Frankly, I wouldn't know how to run this company . . . if I didn't have diversity of thought. We are a very international company and therefore we need an international group of executives."

This is a big challenge for global companies and often involves leapfrogging or accelerating the careers of people from other countries to create real diversity at senior levels. We have watched many executive committees make incomplete or even poor decisions about diverse markets and people because they simply lacked sufficient diversity in their conversations and perceptions. This further flaws the decision making at the top of large, hierarchical global companies that already have difficulty obtaining open and honest feedback; their leaders find it easy to convince themselves the world is pretty much as they decide it is.

5. *Use your head to integrate experiences through cross-cultural and cross-generational training and reading.*

Many leaders can benefit from intense training experience on managing cultural differences, combining cultural self-awareness from self-assessments with reflection on global team experiences and foreign assignments. The combination helps them learn to lead and work in a global environment. We conduct intense action learning experiences for senior leaders at McDonald's and many other companies. A component of these programs is immersion in different cultures, or at least understanding cultural differences. Leaders realize how culture can define what is appropriate leadership and how their cultural background shapes how they view appropriate performance.

Several fascinating studies have been done on intergenerational differences, but few companies offer intergenerational training programs. In many leadership programs we conduct, we ask senior leaders to listen to a panel of high-talent Millennials who are having a conversation about the company in another room, and cannot be seen. Quite often, executives gasp and laugh at the candor and truth of what they are hearing. We then invite the Millennials into the room to debrief together with the executives. This simple experience of learning together how each sees the world creates real insight—and often leads to changed behavior.

6. *Use your head to design and implement management and reward systems that are motivating to varied groups of people.*

Most companies rely on measurement, motivation, and reward systems that focus on equity or "one size fits all." Baby Boomers facing retirement, young parents balancing work and family, and people who want to work part-time frequently find traditional organizations can't accommodate diverse lifestyles and life stages. A challenge for leaders seeking to lead everyone is to become more creative in human resource policies such as flextime, semiretirement, reverse mentoring, sabbaticals, and other more responsive and flexible approaches to managing performance and people.

7. *Use your guts to make tough trade-off decisions.*

Managers ultimately need to test what they have learned in a real leadership situation. They will need to be posted to another country or given responsibility for a global team where tough trade-off decisions must be made based on conflicting values, beliefs, and cultural traditions. They may also need to deal with the demands or recommendations of a young high-potential task force that has a very different view of how the organization should be run or the kind of organizational culture best suited to enable the company to compete or to retain its best talent.

While it is important to be sensitive to different beliefs and traditions, the real test of cross-cultural and intergenerational leadership is in those situations that require a choice between the "right" of one perspective and the equally legitimate needs of someone from a different belief system. These are the crucibles from which future global leaders emerge. In our experience, those leaders who have encountered these differences and worked them through to resolution develop conflict management skills that serve them well across a variety of situations.

8. *Use your heart to fashion a multigenerational organizational culture.*

In the next few years, as the Millennial generation moves into organizations and the Baby Boomers cannot afford to move out, three generations will be living together—Boomers, Gen Xers, and Millennials. Organizations will need to build cultures that value and integrate these different perspectives.

Boomers bring great perspective and experience to an organization, but obviously the ones you need to keep are those who have made adjustments to the vast changes in technology and speed that have occurred during their working life. Gen Xers contribute the new social consciousness discussed in Chapter Eight, and Millennials demand collaboration and trust at a level that has not been evident in the past. The corporate cultures that succeed in the future will be those that leverage multigenerational perspectives and skills and incorporate the expertise of the past, the agility of technology, a wide range of stakeholder interests, and the ability to integrate people to work together through collaboration and trust.

This will require whole leaders who are sensitive to all the differences that these generations represent (heart) while forging them into a winning formula for the marketplace (head) and making tough trade-offs necessary to ensure that the best of each generation is leveraged and the weaknesses are minimized (guts).

These steps should enable managers to develop a new comfort level with diversity, while simultaneously understanding how different needs can be brought together for competitive advantage. The Japanese used to say that when it comes to competitive advantage, you can buy talent and you can buy technology, but you cannot buy a successful corporate culture—it has to be built—and this may be the opportunity to create one that will constitute a competitive advantage.

9. *Use your guts to hold people accountable.*

No matter their generation, their background, or their values, people require accountability to drive performance in organizations. Many leaders confuse generational value differences with expectations around this issue. Even Millennials consistently say, "accommodate our values, but hold us accountable for performance." Some leaders compromise around performance in order to accommodate differing values—a mistake that makes everyone resentful.

WHOLE LEADERSHIP QUESTIONS TO ASK YOURSELF ABOUT LEARNING TO LEAD EVERYONE

Use Your Head

- Do you know what it's like to be from your own culture and how you're different from other cultures?
- How open are you to learning about important differences among the people you lead?
- Are you where you need to be in terms of understanding how differences in culture, generation, nationality, and other factors affect the success of your organization?
- How much time do you spend figuring out how to successfully implement diversity in your organization?
- Do you spend time learning about other cultures?

Use Your Heart

- Have you had experiences that exposed you to other cultures, nationalities, and generations? What did you learn?
- Do you appreciate other cultures, nationalities, and generations?
- How would your colleagues describe you in terms of sensitivity to cultural, national, and generational differences?
- Are you currently mentoring or being mentored by someone from another culture, nationality, or generation?
- Do you demonstrate your understanding and appreciation of differences to others? How?
- Do you know how to motivate employees from different generations?

Use Your Guts

- Does your organization truly reflect the cultures in which you operate?
- How diverse is your leadership team? Does the composition of your team reflect the cultures of your customers?

- Are you able to make the tough trade-offs between cultural sensitivity and maintaining ethical standards?
- Do you know the differences between showing cultural sensitivity and capitulating to cultural norms?
- Do you know where you would draw the line when it comes to accommodating differences?

Become Stakeholder Savvy

I N A RECENT INTERVIEW, SIR MARTIN SORRELL OF WPP DESCRIBED the challenges of leading large organizations in today's world. He told Matthew Gwyther, "These days, complexity goes with the territory. Anybody who believes that life is going to become simpler in this day and age needs to have their head examined. . . . The twenty-first century is not for tidy minds."

When organizational leaders look beyond their walls, what they see is by turns frightening, exciting, and incomprehensible. The perfect storm we have described is a swirl of responsibilities, a series of significant social issues and external stakeholder requirements that are dizzying in their scope and complexity. Leaders must concern themselves not just with a single stakeholder but with a varied and changing set of interest groups and regulatory bodies. External stakeholders have multiplied, not just in number and diversity but in importance to any global organization. To understand how confusing the ever-widening circle of stakeholder responsibility is, consider the common items on the agendas of many executive teams:

- Access to information has given customers power they have never had before, and a senior leadership team must now respond to informed expectations from customers about price, quality, service, product features, potential liability, and warranties, to name a few. The customer now has a seat at the executive conference table, in one way or another.

- Regulators, and the politicians who pick them, are a constant factor in decision making because they are more conservative, require much more data, have the power to shut down operations, delay product launches, or request privileged information. Regulators require executive teams to make sure that everyone is in compliance with relevant statutes and policies; at the same time, these leaders must maintain their appetite for risk and innovation.

- Global supply chains require constant investment attention, vigilance, and redesign. Despite wild fluctuations in the price of oil, companies are becoming more dependent on global distribution—often outsourcing functions around the globe and becoming heavily dependent on suppliers not just in manufacturing and procurement but also in customer service, market research, and HR support centers. These outsourced groups can be located anywhere in the world—as long as they are cheap and efficient.

- Expectations for quarterly results from investors force trade-off decisions that emphasize short- over long-term investments. The relentless pressure for growth and profitability in companies where selling, general, and administrative expenses have been cut to the bone requires renewed discipline around prioritization and execution.

- Emerging markets represent a huge opportunity and a real threat. Most executive teams today are spending a lot of time considering how to grow in other markets while parrying the nontraditional competitors who are emerging in every industry. Even in very sophisticated industries—medical devices, technology, computers, pharmaceuticals—emerging market competitors are now entering developed markets with quality products at lower cost. Executives scan what's happening and develop the nimbleness to respond quickly to new threats, while preparing for increasing competition. Most teams have realized that Thomas Friedman is right—the world *is* flat around outsourcing, but so is the competitive playing field, with few advantages to the home team.

- Ethical issues dominate discussions due to advances in neurotechnology, biotechnology, and nanotechnology, creating concerns among consumer groups around the world for simultaneous consumer protection from these advances and consumer access to the same advances.

These external forces represent rapidly multiplying stakeholder constituencies. This diversity of interests must be taken into account in corporate policy decisions. They also raise a particularly vexing issue: pressure on leaders to act in socially responsible ways while maintaining shareholder value.

TURNING GREEN WITHOUT TURNING RED: THE ENVIRONMENTALIST AND THE SHAREHOLDER

Imagine the thought process of a leader confronting the challenge of behaving in a socially responsible way while still delivering shareholder value:

THOUGHT #1: We have a great opportunity to do business in China; we found a supplier that will help us reduce our costs significantly.

THOUGHT #2: Just got slammed in the media because our supplier's products contain high amounts of lead. Will switch to supplier in South Korea with great reputation for quality.

THOUGHT #3: Being boycotted by U.S. consumer groups protesting sweatshop conditions at our South Korea supplier. Will move everything to our plants in the United States and Canada.

THOUGHT #4: Just received a low rating because of the high carbon emissions of our North American plants. We'll divest ourselves of all our manufacturing facilities and contract the work out.

THOUGHT #5: Our divestiture is under investigation by a regulatory body that has told us it has found financial irregularities in how we structured the divestiture.

THOUGHT #6: Our main competitor is killing us because of his low-cost, high-quality Chinese manufacturing facilities. We realize we have a great opportunity if we do business in China.

That sequence is only slightly tongue-in-cheek. Complexity isn't particularly funny to leaders trying to sort through the contradictions, paradoxes, and ambiguities that come with just about any major decision and the effort to be sure that actions are taken in a socially responsible way.

There is an ongoing debate about what role corporations should take in addressing important social issues. Last year, the *Economist* described both sides. On one hand are people like Robert Reich, labor secretary under Bill Clinton, arguing that corporations' desire to be socially responsible diverts them from the more realistic and important task of getting governments to solve social problems. On the other side of the debate are people like Simon Zadek, head of a corporate social responsibility (CSR) lobby group, saying that the debate is over and it's only a question of what companies do and how they do it, not whether they should.

More attention than ever is being given to this issue. The 2007 State of Corporate Citizenship Survey conducted by the Boston College Center for Corporate Citizenship surveyed more than seven hundred top executives. These executives acknowledged a growing distrust of large corporations having to do with everything from excessive CEO pay packages to perceived lack of accountability to lack of public understanding of what companies actually do to stories of corruption to the recent crisis in sub-prime mortgages. Part of the response to these negative perceptions has been for senior executives to increase their focus on social responsibility. However, the study found that while many companies have publicly embraced the need to step up involvement in providing solutions to social problems, there is a big gap between what they say they value and what they actually do. Less than half the companies surveyed have incorporated good corporate citizenship into their business planning process or corporate policies, even though more than three-quarters said this was a priority.

To complicate this picture further, most companies acknowledge that they don't really understand their customers' or employees' expectations when it comes to CSR. A global study by IBM has recently reinforced the importance of this issue. Over half of the companies expressed the view that CSR represents an opportunity for revenue generation and competitive advantage and was not just a regulatory or philanthropic effort. George Pohle, VP of IBM's Business Consulting Practice, said, "It's not only critical for businesses to keep up with the emerging demands of their stakeholders, but to build CSR into the core of their business strategy. That way CSR is not viewed as a discretionary cost but an investment that will bring financial returns. And since customers are changing buying behavior as a result of CSR, the financial impact can be dramatic."

The United States is not the only place where these issues are prominent. Since 2002, more than 250 businesses in the United Kingdom have been using the Business in the Community Corporate Responsibility Index as a management tool. Last year's results showed a trend toward seeing responsible business as a competitive advantage and increasing evidence that social and environmental issues were influencing decision making. Nevertheless, significant challenges were identified when it came to thoroughly embedding practices, policies, behaviors, and values consistently across the breadth and depth of an organization.

Even organizations that seem to have a handle on managing stakeholder diversity get thrown for a loop. Apple has long enjoyed a reputation as a progressive, innovative, and employee-centric company. Yet in June 2007, an environmental group, Climate Counts, published a report ranking companies on their actions related to greenhouse gases. Apple scored 2 out of 100 (with 1 being the lowest score). Expectations are increasing for companies to improve energy efficiency and reduce greenhouse gas emissions—and companies that fail to meet those expectations face potentially serious business consequences.

Even for a company like Apple, it's tough to keep an eye on everything. And even if you can keep an eye on everything, the trade-offs between profitability and social responsibility are enormously difficult to measure.

We have moved a long way from the 1970s, when environmental groups were considered "pesky activists." Today it is the big pension funds, state controllers, and institutional investors that are demanding that companies have an environmental conscience that gets translated into budget and company priorities. In a recent global survey by BearingPoint regarding green and sustainable supply chains, 83 percent of corporate respondents reported that they have adopted environmental strategies to protect brand image and to address environmental regulations.

Ecological Concerns

Global warming, oil prices, rising insurance rates due to environmental trends, pollution problems in increasingly industrialized Russia and China, and many other factors have forced leaders to consider environmental concerns more seriously. It's not just that environmental issues are having a greater impact on organizations—leaders are being forced to make difficult decisions about them. What level of responsibility do CEOs have? How much should they do to reduce their company's carbon footprint, and at what cost to the bottom line? As the price of oil rises, what should you do about your supply chain that reaches around the world? Can you still afford to manufacture in one place and transport the product to another location? And more subtly, will any of these problems actually manifest themselves on your watch?

What adds even more to the complexity is that no one is quite sure how serious these issues are. Are we talking about the sustainability of resources like water? Are we talking about the long-term survival of the planet? And if your company is a major contributor to a problem, does your responsibility go beyond social? Jeffrey Sachs, former Harvard professor and adviser to leaders in emerging governments, believes the situation demands the attention of leaders at every level throughout the world. He observes that life on the planet as we know it faces fundamental threats from a combination of water reservoir depletion, population growth, and lack of renewable energy—all of which will stifle economic expansion and have important market, political, and social ramifications within current lifetimes.

In other words, as awareness of environmental problems increases, so too may awareness of how your company is contributing to these problems. You may discover that people—especially young people— don't want to work for your organization. You may find yourself the subject of a boycott. You may discover that you're the target of a consumer activist group. So you have social and business reasons to become concerned about the environment and deal with your part of the environmental problems. The catch, of course, is that since these are by definition long-term problems, if you spend too much time and money dealing with them, you may face short-term pressure from Wall Street or shareholders.

Regulatory Stakeholders

Anyone who has dealt with a regulatory agency recently knows how much additional work it now takes to remain in compliance. Part of the problem, especially in the United States, is that the regulations have become incredibly complex. Sarbanes-Oxley is just one piece of legislation that has cost organizations billions and often requires rethinking and restructuring of policies and practices. Alan Greenspan, the former Federal Reserve chairman, was quoted in a *Financial Times* article as saying, "What worries me is that the regulatory system is by its very nature creating less flexibility . . . we need to create flexibility so we can absorb shocks in a manner that does not destabilize the system." The U.S. sub-prime mortgage bubble that precipitated a global credit crisis also precipitated demands for more regulation, controls, and oversight—which may not be inappropriate, but will increase regulatory control.

Earlier, we used the word *compliance,* which is a common response to regulatory bodies. Yet we're moving from a compliance mind-set to a responsibility perspective, and the latter is a much more complex notion. With compliance, you know specifically what you have to do to "pass." With responsibility, you're dealing with a much vaguer concept that involves a much greater range of action. If you're responsible, do you close your mildly polluting plant in Mexico because of excess capacity, even though you may be on the brink of a major strike? And if you close it and put hundreds of Mexicans out of work, is that being responsible on a local level?

To be seen as responsible today requires establishing your own standards that sometimes exceed local regulations. GE, for example, has chosen to build new plants to world standards, not local standards, whether in Mexico or China. The rationale: world-standard plants are more efficient and therefore provide cost advantages; they ensure better health and safety standards for employees, making the plant more competitive in the constant search for global talent, and they avoid future retooling costs to meet high environmental regulatory standards that will be inevitable. Johnson & Johnson, because of its corporate credo, also upholds global standards for safety, cleanliness, compliance, and quality, no matter the country in which its people are doing business. Its leaders see this as both managing for the long term and upholding their role as global citizens who operate with the highest standards. They've discovered it's good business, reflecting positively on their brand, attracting the best employees, and ensuring the confidence of customers around the world.

Despite the pressures of economic downturns, leaders are starting to view compliance as an internal responsibility rather than external requirement. Well-managed companies are moving from regulations to ethics, and the discussion at the executive level is increasingly not about regulatory risk from a compliance perspective but about regulatory risk from an ethical perspective. Many executives are asking, "How efficient are the cars in our fleet?" and "How well are we doing at controlling our own emissions?" They're asking these questions from a sense of personal responsibility. Regulatory risk has moved from the government to the executive teams and now to the vision and values of leaders.

Consumer Activism and Networking

Consumers also have much to say about corporate responsibility. Unlike the past, when consumer activities were confined to NGOs and nonprofit organizations, today's consumers have taken things into their own hands and are operating independently to express their concerns about the environment. From Prius and other hybrid automobile choices to examining labels on consumer products to reading and digesting blogs about carbon emissions, product content, and supervisory practices around the globe, consumers today are scrutinizing companies as never before.

And they don't want to pay more for their principles. A BMW spokesperson recently said the company felt trapped in a twenty-first-century Catch-22—how to make its high-performance cars more efficient and boost profits at the same time. BMW was caught off guard by the popularity of Toyota and Lexus hybrid models and is trying to catch up, but it is finding that the required R&D spending can't be passed on to consumers.

Generational differences are also having an impact. As noted, Millennials are connected—perhaps the most team-oriented, collegial group in decades. This means they care what other people think and they care about the impact they have on others. Their social consciousness combined with their reflexive connecting abilities mean they are constantly comparing ideas and viewpoints about everything from Green companies to corporate gender policies.

Everything Is Related to Everything Else—and Moving Fast

We were with the CEO of a major media organization recently, and he told us he used to be able to apply his analytical abilities to make key decisions, but he can't do that anymore because too many factors impact organizational performance and external markets. He admitted that it was impossible to stay on top of any issue since everything from technology to consumer tastes is changing so quickly.

The complexity of creating a sound strategy is staggering. Few strategies remain viable for long because during the time of a perfect storm, nothing stays the same for long. New technologies, customer preferences, and economic trends blow through businesses regularly. Health care research provides a paradigm for how you can't bank on anything for long. Typically, a university group announces a new discovery about cancer, heart disease, or some other malady. Much excitement surrounds this "breakthrough" and a slew of approaches go into the development pipeline to respond. Six months later a new study is released that contradicts the earlier study.

It used to be that a company could bring out a new product and be reasonably sure of the size of the market, the need the product met among a targeted group, and what competitors offered. It could also be reasonably sure that everything it knew would hold true for at least a few years. Today, competitors come out of nowhere overnight; customers sour almost as quickly on a product that they once embraced. As a result, relying on traditional research to introduce a product has become a game where the odds are stacked against you. Acting with insufficient data has become a leadership skill.

It seems as though interdependence is making it impossible to decide anything without considering multiple, far-reaching ramifications. The days of individual problem solving are over. In the old days, one of your suppliers' factory managers in a province of China could solve a quality problem in any way he saw fit without worrying about external stakeholders. It might result in more lead in toys, or bacteria in food products, but no one was watching. Today, if that solution results in a problem that doesn't meet U.S. regulatory standards, your company may be the subject of a congressional investigation. It is difficult to make decisions in isolation, no matter where you are. If these choices are significant enough, they're bound to be felt and responded to by everyone from foreign governments to consumer activist groups to regulatory bodies.

Some Get It Right; Others Don't

Some companies are responding adroitly to environmental issues at surprising levels of commitment. Coca-Cola and the World Wildlife

Fund are tackling water quality issues; McDonald's and Greenpeace are working to mitigate deforestation; Clorox and the Sierra Club are working together on developing a new green product line.

Ten years ago corporate responsibility (CR) was a concept on the sidelines at Nike. When activists were critical of Nike for labor practices in contract factories around the world, Nike was ill-equipped to see the signals, not well prepared to engage in meaningful dialogue with key stakeholders, and unable to take key steps to remedy, as much as possible, the issues.

Now, things are very different. Nike has embraced CR as a genuine catalyst for innovation. Nike's aim is to embed positive environmental, social, and labor conditions in the heart of its business. The goal is ultimately to showcase a successful company built on the foundation of social innovation. This transformation has been a long and, at times, difficult journey. But Nike has changed its CR approach from a risk management mindset to one of innovation and business integration. For example, two years ago Nike revealed where the 700 contract factories employing around 800,000 people in fifty-two countries were located. The move was an effort to help raise standards and encourage further industry transparency and collaboration, while also seeking to continue to improve conditions for contract factory workers.

Other companies have not met challenges as successfully. Wal-Mart has struggled as its business has become more complex. It has a lot riding on its ability to succeed in Japan, where it has partnered with Seiyu, acquiring 51 percent of the company. Early on, Wal-Mart convinced Seiyu management to dismiss 25 percent of its headquarters staff. No doubt Wal-Mart was simply following its standard operating procedure, and the cut made perfect fiscal sense from a numbers perspective. What Wal-Mart may not have considered, however, is how this move would be interpreted in Japan and observed throughout the rest of the world. It's unusual for large numbers of people to be downsized out of jobs in that country. More significant, perhaps, it opened Wal-Mart to accusations that it was trying to "Americanize" a Japanese company. Wal-Mart also didn't seem to anticipate that its strategy of "always low prices" wasn't well suited to the Japanese market, where many people are willing to pay top dollar for high-quality goods and services. In short, Wal-Mart was tripped up by the complexity of doing business in Japan.

Whole Leadership and Becoming a Stakeholder-Savvy Leader

Leaders at the forefront in dealing with diverse stakeholder concerns understand that they must ask uncomfortable questions—questions that will challenge them and their organizations even though they may create further complexity and uncertainty. But the answer is not to evade or ignore the unpleasant. Turning green without turning red requires a tough reality check and can only be done with a full understanding and open debate of both sides of an issue—ethical and financial. To balance all these demands, whole leaders know they have to use their head to analyze the trade-offs, their heart to identify with the needs of different constituencies, and their guts to make the difficult decisions that will determine the kind of company they lead, what their company stands for, and what they will be known for as a leader.

Many people today are beginning to talk about "socially responsible leadership." Socially responsible leaders go beyond fulfilling the minimal obligations of compliance to show concern about issues beyond their own organization and ask hard, long-term questions when making business decisions. Whole leaders work to become socially responsible leaders by becoming stakeholder savvy by taking the steps shown in Figure 8.1.

1. *Use your head to determine which social issues are important to achieving your company vision—as both threats and opportunities.*

As noted, many special interest groups exist and their numbers are increasing all the time. Determine which of these groups is most relevant—as a threat or an opportunity—to the future vision your company has of itself. In many instances, this will require using your head to look beyond the current situation and see new possibilities for cooperation and collaboration superseding traditional hostilities and confrontational relationships. It means moving beyond a siege mentality to look creatively at how what appear to be conflicting interests can be transcended, as the examples of Coca-Cola, McDonald's, and Clorox demonstrate.

2. *Use your heart to reach out to relevant global networks of stakeholders, both friendly and hostile.*

Reaching out to relevant stakeholders requires finding the channels through which dialogues can be most productively undertaken

FIGURE 8.1. *Become Stakeholder Savvy.*

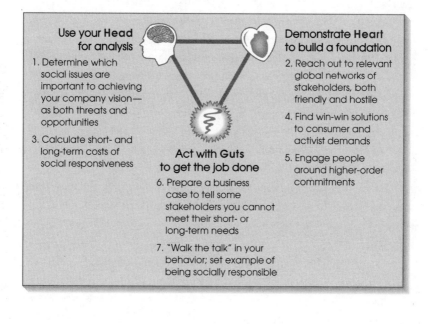

Use your Head for analysis

1. Determine which social issues are important to achieving your company vision—as both threats and opportunities

3. Calculate short- and long-term costs of social responsiveness

Act with Guts to get the job done

6. Prepare a business case to tell some stakeholders you cannot meet their short- or long-term needs

7. "Walk the talk" in your behavior; set example of being socially responsible

Demonstrate Heart to build a foundation

2. Reach out to relevant global networks of stakeholders, both friendly and hostile

4. Find win-win solutions to consumer and activist demands

5. Engage people around higher-order commitments

and the forums through which ongoing cooperation and discussion can be carried out. This may not be readily apparent and may take some careful consideration. Some formal forums may already have been established, including association or industry initiatives. In other cases you may need to find brokers who can help find common ground with stakeholders who are important to you, but who may initially be hostile to the idea of collaborative action. Bank of America regularly meets with consumer activist groups such as Hispanic customers or inner-city coalitions. Use of these forums can deepen your understanding of the concerns, viewpoints, and issues that are relevant to your stakeholders. You may not agree with everything you hear, but you can be sure that your stakeholders want to be heard.

3. *Use your head to calculate short- and long-term costs of social responsiveness.*

Once you have met with various groups and understand their perspectives and their demands, conduct a total review of the short- and long-term costs of adopting strategies that are responsive to different cohorts. It is obvious that you will not be able to satisfy everyone, so gathering together the best analysis will be critical to the next step. This is the only way you'll be able to make trade-offs. Remember that the question is not whether to be socially responsible (that debate is over), it's how and where. You also need to have both a short-term and a long-term view. Many of the opportunities for generating revenues and increasing competitiveness will not materialize overnight. You may be able to achieve some quick wins, but you must have the long view as well.

4. *Use your heart to find win-win solutions to consumer and activist demands.*

Now that you know the parameters within which you can work, return to the negotiating table with those groups where a win-win solution is possible. These conversations need to be conducted within the context of all your values and concerns for all stakeholders globally and should reflect a total organization perspective worldwide, rather than a piecemeal approach by country, region, product, or business.

5. *Use your heart to engage people around higher-order commitments.*

Engaging employees with the values of community, inspiring them to take personal action on the environment, and discovering what people care about for the future are ways to build socially responsible organizations. Leaders today must listen to what employees care about and create an environment that employees find purposeful and inspiring. This is true for both altruistic and competitive reasons. When it comes to finding, keeping, and retaining talent, studies of Millennial and Gen Y employees cite "working for an organization I can be proud of" as high on the list of key motivators.

6. *Use your guts to prepare a business case to tell some stakeholders you cannot meet their short- or long-term needs.*

The reality is that you will not be able to offer a win-win solution for many of the groups you interact with. For each of these, develop a business case for why you are unable to meet their demands and prepare a strategy for dealing with them in the short and long term. This should be done within an overall strategic stakeholder plan that should be updated annually so that all your senior managers understand your position regarding the many demands that are made on the organization around the world.

7. Use your guts to "walk the talk" in your behavior and set an example of being socially responsible.

People watch leaders to discern their true values. Many leaders express concern about the environment but don't curtail their own carbon emissions. They declare their company is "green" but don't back it up with tougher standards for emissions and energy use, and they don't offer flextime to reduce commuting or make investments in green technologies. Today, many people recognize that being seen as "green" can be an advantage, but employees and consumers are quick to recognize whether these statements are authentic or not. The test is behavior, not rhetoric.

WHOLE LEADERSHIP QUESTIONS TO ASK YOURSELF TO BECOME STAKEHOLDER SAVVY

Use Your Head

- What environmental impact will your major decisions have—not only in the near term but in the long term?
- What are the major opportunities for becoming more socially responsible?
- How can you generate more revenue and beat your competition by being more socially responsible?
- If your company is to be seen as an environmentally responsible corporate citizen, what standards need to be applied to your behavior worldwide?

Use Your Heart

- Who are your key stakeholders when it comes to social responsibility, and what do they care about?
- Are you actively involved in conversations with your stakeholders about issues of social responsibility? What are you learning?
- How actively engaged are your people in conversations about social responsibility? Should you be doing more?
- What will you say to stockholders to explain your decision to be a responsible leader in the world community? What values and vision will you describe that will strike a chord with them and still reflect your true beliefs?

Use Your Guts

- How do you make sure that your team is aligned on issues of social responsibility? Are they willing to make the same commitment you are?

- Are you having the tough conversations with stakeholders about what you can and can't do when it comes to social responsibility?

- Can you afford to have one set of standards in one part of the world and another set somewhere else? How much variation can you allow before you are seen as being opportunistic or hypocritical?

- What investment will be required to ensure that you meet environmental concerns beyond what is required simply for compliance?

Section Three: Navigating the Wave of Uncertainty

HENRY KISSINGER IS REPORTED TO HAVE SAID THAT THE WORLD would look back on the Cold War as the most stable time of the twentieth century. Two superpowers competing for everything with the power of mutual destruction constituted an ironically restful balance. But with the dissolution of the Soviet Union, the fall of the Berlin Wall, the emergence of China, India, and Middle Eastern sovereign wealth funds, the subsequent reemergence of Russia and the wild card threat of bio and nuclear terrorism, the twenty-first century has become filled with a plethora of new economic, political, and military powerhouses that have created a much more unstable world.

Welcome to the third wave of the perfect storm—uncertainty. And uncertainty is not only created by these global changes. It has also been exacerbated by the first two waves: complexity and diversity, multiplied by technology, have meant that leaders today must deal with enormous uncertainty. The odds of being right have diminished, risk has increased, complex paradoxes have emerged, and leaders are now thrust into making decisions with consequences never before imagined.

In this world, captains who limit their tools will find navigating the perfect storm an almost impossible challenge. Leaders need to use every capacity in their head, heart, and guts to successfully navigate the wave of uncertainty. But an overriding theme of successfully navigating uncertainty is a leader's courage to stand for clear vision and values. The perfect storm is ultimately a challenge of character.

Leaders must draw on their self-knowledge and values to steer a course when others around them are confused and afraid. The perfect storm is not a time for the timid or inexperienced.

In Chapter Nine we look at how whole leaders approach risk and uncertainty. In Chapter Ten we provide a way to balance the paradoxes of a complex and conflict-ridden world of right versus right. And in Chapter Eleven we delve into the process by which whole leaders clarify their values and what they will have the courage to stand for. The perfect storm does not demand perfect captains, but it does demand captains who are aware of their strengths and weaknesses and able to use their crew's skills and abilities to navigate through uncertain waters.

CHAPTER 9

Redefine Risk and Uncertainty

WINSTON CHURCHILL ONCE OBSERVED, "TRUE GENIUS RESIDES in the capacity for evaluation of uncertain, hazardous, and conflicting information." Unfortunately, most of us are not geniuses. And very few of us "embrace uncertainty" as many experts on the subject have counseled. Nonetheless, that may be the first necessary step in successfully dealing with risk and uncertainty.

As difficult as it is to do, as a leader you must accept and even embrace a certain level of risk and uncertainty in your business—risk that a valued direct report could leave the company unexpectedly, risk that your brand can suffer from product liability, or an important project can be late or go off track, or your market share can plummet suddenly. Between 1993 and 2004, almost 50 percent of the Fortune 500 experienced a drop in market value greater than 30 percent lasting more than twelve months, and 30 percent experienced a lasting drop greater than 60 percent. There are real dangers for companies and leaders, and a real likelihood of uneasiness, instability, and uncertainty. The trick is for leaders to find a comfort level operating in the space between chaos and control, and to redefine risk as opportunity.

Most CEOs agree that certainty and uncertainty have an optimum level—and every business and every level of every business has to determine the best space to play in. Generally the lower you work in an organization the more certainty you need for excellence of execution, but the higher you are the more uncertainty you must tolerate to ensure you are scanning a wide enough horizon of possibilities and looking for opportunities in risks.

We live and work in a time of growing uncertainty caused by everything from increased information flow to an interconnected global marketplace, technological change, and global warming. The insurance industry is in a state of upheaval as it has thrown out its old computer models of risk, generated in a time when radical weather patterns happened "once every hundred years." The hundred-year storms and droughts now seem to be appearing every few years, creating enormous financial strains and confusion. But in the middle of this unprecedented risk, as always, some companies and leaders have found new opportunities. New products and services are being introduced: "green building property insurance," for instance, which pays the cost of replacing recyclable materials, recertification of environmental conformity, and coverage of physical damage or equipment breakdown of renewable energy projects.

Business decisions are riskier in this uncertain climate—low-risk decisions from five or ten years ago are now medium-risk, and medium-risk ones are now high-risk. It used to be that good analysis done within a stable environment would virtually ensure low-risk decision making. Today, though that analysis is still necessary, it ensures nothing. You can do the most rigorous analysis in the world and be blindsided by a hundred different unexpected events—a new competitor from a developing market, a spike in commodity prices or shortage of supply, the sudden collapse of a key partner, or—as many CEOs tell us—"someone, somewhere, doing something dumb." In fact, many leaders believe the greatest threat to any company is the risk management group, because it gives everyone a false sense of being able to prevent the unpreventable!

OPERATIONAL, STRATEGIC, AND PERSONAL RISK

Risk for most organizations means financial and operational risk. Our colleague Adrian Slywotzky has written an excellent book, *The Upside,* in which he expands the concept of risk from financial and operational risk to areas of "strategic risk." He defines seven different areas: risks to an entire industry, technology risks, brand risks, competitor risks, consumer risks, the risks of project failure, and the risk of stagnation due to price or volume declines or a weakening product pipeline. Slywotzky argues that these strategic (rather than financial or operational) risks should be examined not only as threats but as opportunities for innovation and redefining the nature of the competitive game being played. He cites steps leaders can take to mitigate different types of strategic risk, such as "double betting" or funding two or more approaches to technology development. Brand risk can be reduced by the range of methods you use to build and communicate your brand, and the risks of customer shifts to other sources can be reduced by collecting more proprietary information about your customers and using it to deepen their relationship with your company.

Mindy Grossman, CEO of HSN (formerly Home Shopping Network), observes that in an uncertain environment filled with risks and opportunities, good leaders have to hedge in many ways, including backing up projects with additional research, or putting more and different products in front of customers to lower the dependence on a few blockbusters. Pharmaceutical company executives routinely hedge their drug pipeline with complex financial forecasts in an effort to reduce the effects of regulatory rejection of compounds.

But we can broaden the definition of leadership risk. It's not just organizational risk that must be considered, but individual risk as well. While your organization may have a certain risk profile in relationship to the seven categories just mentioned, psychological testing has revealed that all leaders have their own individual risk profiles called derailers. We have detailed these risk factors in an earlier book, *Why CEOs Fail*. As a leader, you may have a great capacity to work effectively in stable conditions and take significant risks there, but you may respond to uncertainty by overplaying your strengths, which then become your risk factors or derailers. Your personal strengths and weaknesses and your tolerance for risk and ambiguity may be very different from those of other managers in your organization—or in the industry. There is more than one story to be told about how a CEO was willing to "gamble the company" on a bet that paid off while people who were "overly cautious" sat fearfully by.

Some leaders are acutely aware of project risks, for instance, but oblivious to their personal risk profile. They haven't engaged in the reflection required to understand their biases and unquestioned assumptions. They may not realize that hubris prevents them from thinking long and hard before taking a risk. They may not understand that they're *pleasers,* and that taking risks often thwarts their desire to please, and so they refrain from taking even smart gambles.

The research on leadership bias in mergers and acquisitions shows that many leaders undertaking acquisitions have an inflated sense of self and pursue targeted companies with great hubris. Despite some clear data on the general failure of most acquisitions to achieve growth targets, their bias is that they can succeed where others can't. This makes them vulnerable to premature or rushed decision making. Paul Shoemaker has summed up the problem as leaders who have "myopic eyes" (limited sensors of risk) or are "timid souls" (lacking the self-confidence to intuit what needs to be done).

Other managers respond to uncertainty by trying to control risks—and also get in trouble. To a certain extent, this desire to control risk is inevitable, a result of management's traditional need to create order out of chaos. Until relatively recently organizations have been able to achieve a modicum of order. Now, though, a certain amount of chaos is inevitable. However, in an ironic twist, Salanick and Meindl have found that many leaders attribute good quarters of company performance to internal factors that they control, while in bad quarters they tend to blame external factors. While this is probably not untrue, our guess is that the perception of what is "in control" and "out of control" may be one clue as to some managers' success in dealing with risk and uncertainty.

DEGREES OF UNCERTAINTY

How leaders perceive risk and uncertainty is important. Studies have shown that leaders vary greatly in their tolerance for uncertainty. Bill Weldon, CEO of Johnson & Johnson, has observed that in order to manage risk, leaders have to be able to endure some degree of chaos until the right course of action appears. Harvard professor Ron Heifetz has written in *Leadership Without Easy Answers* that leaders have to endure chaos and uncertainty in order to create a "pressure cooker" in which people find their own answers and solve problems— rather than delegating upward to the leader to solve everything.

In *Embracing Uncertainty,* Phillip Clampitt and Robert DeKoch define a spectrum of uncertainty that begins with "laws" at the certainty end and continues to "the unknown" at the uncertainty end. In between are what they call "principles, rules of thumb, hunches and intuitions," all of which have degrees of certainty attached to them. In today's fact-based world, most companies are working to get away from the unknowns, intuition, and hunches and develop as many rules of thumb, principles, and laws, or at least fact-based experiences, as possible. Whenever possible, "gut instincts" are replaced with authorities, experiences, reasoning, and testing. But real uncertainty takes leaders into the realm of hunches, intuition, and "gut instincts"—and a mind-set that encourages a Zen-like questioning like "what wants to happen here?"

How to Take Risks When Uncertainty Is Everywhere

What we're suggesting is that you reflect on and communicate how you feel about risk. Creating your own personal and organizational approach to risk will help you become aware of the biases and assumptions that lurk beneath the surface. George Day and Paul Shoemaker describe this as "vigilance." They maintain that a vigilant leader has a heightened state of awareness of threats and opportunities even with limited information. In a study of 119 global companies, they identified vigilance of the leadership as the most important driver of "organizational peripheral vision" or the ability to see around corners and into the future to anticipate what could happen. The scope of your vision and scanning ultimately determines the vigilance of your organization—the speed with which it perceives new risks and opportunities. Until you articulate the role that uncertainty and risk play in your business and your own leadership, you may be operating as a partial leader when it comes to risk.

Uncertainty triggers a conditioned response to risk. The more unpredictable or chaotic the situation, the more likely that you'll respond to risk reflexively, doing what you always have done. When you bring your assumptions about certainty and risk to conscious attention, you give yourself a chance to examine and amend them. Are the assumptions that informed your approach last year still valid?

What have you learned that has stretched your willingness to take risks and to see opportunities in uncertainty in a new way? How will you challenge yourself to ensure you are not reacting with the fateful phrase "we tried that before and . . ."—when "before" was a different time in a different world—so you realize you may need to try something under different circumstances?

WHOLE LEADERSHIP APPROACH TO REDEFINING RISK AND UNCERTAINTY

Some leaders believe they can outthink risk, that they can compartmentalize uncertainty, identifying and controlling it. For this reason, many companies respond to the highly volatile, uncertain conditions of the perfect storm by rearranging the deck chairs—they restructure based on their analysis.

This head approach isn't necessarily the wrong thing to do—but it's an incomplete response. It may feel good because it represents action, and doing something always feels more leaderlike than doing nothing. But it's not enough. What is enough is being aware of and able to use head, heart, and guts capacities in response to uncertainty and risk, as outlined in Figure 9.1.

1. *Use your head to expand your definition of risk.*

Many companies have won handsomely by examining strategic risks and then developing approaches to use them to their advantage. GE has reinvented itself many times through divestiture in industry and asset allocation to a newer, more growth-oriented area. GM used its customer data base to leverage its OnStar subscription service. Many airlines have met the collapse of their industry with partner alliances, code sharing, and collaborations short of merger that have enhanced their reach.

But strategic risk analysis and action, while focusing on a unique set of opportunities that can be dealt with in a broader way, does not replace preparation for financial and operational risks, which should not be overlooked. These require a different kind of preparation, including focus on traditional financial controls and effective processes to reduce variance.

2. *Use your head to create "resilience drills" to practice how you will react to unexpected events.*

FIGURE 9.1. *Redefine Risk and Uncertainty.*

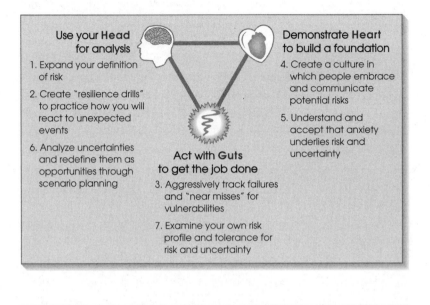

What we call "resilience drills" are critical to the management of risk in today's uncertain environment. Operational risk management poses two basic challenges: the detection and identification of risk, and the development of readiness for response. Resilience drills prepare organizations not only for the containment of a risk but also to restore balance and operational efficiency and effectiveness as soon as possible after an unexpected event.

Some organizations have as their sole purpose the containment of the unexpected and rapid bounce-back from its effects. SWAT teams, fire departments, trauma centers, and other emergency teams practice drills to ensure rapid response to an unexpected event that allows immediate containment while also allowing after-action reviews and the return to normalcy as quickly as possible. These "high resilient organizations," as they have been called, track small failures, stay extremely alert and sensitive to any change that might heighten risk, and reset quickly after a response so they are ready to answer the next call for their services.

In today's work, risk management is not a one-time event; it is increasingly an ongoing part of every company's headquarters effort.

All companies today must therefore have ways of identifying operational and strategic risks, but that is not enough. For each area of risk, you should prepare a "resilience drill" that will ensure that the organization not only contains the risk but manages its way back to normal as quickly as possible. Each organization unit responsible for ensuring the protection of your brand, supply chain, talent, and whatever other range of risks you identify should have a "resilience drill" that can be activated whenever a threat—or potential threat—appears. For example, one HR team we are working with asks and answers, as part of its talent strategy and planning, "What are the risks of large-scale departures through retirements, market downturns, and other calamities?" For almost any business or function where there is a strategy there is also an opportunity to build resilience.

3. *Use your guts to aggressively track failures and "near misses" for vulnerabilities.*

During World War II, Dwight Eisenhower said, "Plans are useless, but planning is essential." In other words, make the cognitive effort to analyze the uncertain situations that may arise and create plans to deal with them, but don't put too much stock in the plans you create. The planning effort itself is what's valuable, since that's where you should be soliciting a diverse range of perspectives from a diverse group of people.

The development of plans is no excuse for relaxing your detection systems, or for failing to constantly reevaluate what constitutes a risk. The greatest risk in risk management is having a completed plan that makes you believe that you have analyzed all possible risks and developed contingency plans to cover yourself. Today, many leaders in financial services and banks are asking, "Where were our risk managers when we were investing in sub-prime credit instruments?" Those same risk managers answer, "We can't be responsible for all institutional risk—that's the job of line managers."

These major failures, such as the recent meltdown of the credit markets, are painful—but offer prime opportunities for learning and new insight. Evaluating near misses and real failures can help you make sure that they do not contain the seeds of unexpected risk in the future. The response to failure is often to lock down against all future risks, as evidenced by the long lines for airport security after the 9/11 terrorist attack, or the tightening of all credit as a response to major bank losses. The trick is to learn from near misses and failures without overcorrecting.

Many organizations have thought something was a one-time occurrence, merely a blip on a screen, only to learn later that it was actually the beginning of a trajectory that was unforeseen because people did not ask aggressive questions about the source of the apparently minor matter. Most people focus instead on being happy that they "got past that one"; in some unfortunate but not atypical cases, they just want to make sure that no one ever knows how close they came to a real failure for the company. This kind of behavior will eventually prove deadly in an uncertain and high-risk environment.

4. *Use your heart to create a culture in which people embrace and communicate potential risks.*

Though using your head means obtaining and analyzing information from a variety of sources, you require heart to bring that information within your grasp. How do you reach out to a sufficient number of people and empower them so they can help you manage an uncertain process? This is the challenge for leaders who have relied on head abilities. Cognitively focused leaders try to do everything themselves, assisted perhaps by a small circle of like-minded individuals. This may work when everything is known and predictable and risks are relatively small, but it doesn't work in today's environment. Today's leaders need to form the relationships that open up fresh avenues of information and ideas. In this way, they not only perceive alternative ways of handling risky, uncertain situations, they enlist a more diverse group in helping them implement solutions.

Of course, no one is going to sign up with a leader who maintains a closed-off, hard-headed demeanor. It's only when you demonstrate humility and even some vulnerability in the midst of uncertainty that you can mobilize a range of people. This is the human response to situations that are dire, confusing, and threatening. It's the type of response that communicates you get it—you feel what others are feeling. It's genuine, and your people will respond when you're authentic.

Bill Weldon communicates his genuine humility during uncertain times by admitting "I don't know" on certain occasions when people ask what should be done. Mark Parker, CEO of Nike, has said publicly, "I'm still learning." Andrea Jung, CEO of Avon, publicly accepted responsibility for Avon's setbacks in 2005. When Dick

Clark took over at Merck, he was coming from the manufacturing side and the media questioned his experience and expertise. He responded that he didn't have all the answers (rather than fight back and pretend to have them) but also communicated exactly how he intended to approach the challenges and uncertain issues facing the company.

People back leaders with heart when they propose risky approaches to difficult problems. They believe in them and support them, and this real support actually lowers the risk. As a leader, when you demonstrate that you do not have all the answers, or even know all the questions, you encourage others to speak up not only to help but also to feel listened to and not fear punishment. In our book *Unnatural Leadership,* we advised leaders to recognize that in many situations acknowledging vulnerability, while seemingly unnatural, is a powerful tool for building commitment and alignment. As we discussed in Chapter Five, driving out fear is a major step in encouraging innovation. It is also necessary for risk management, because without trust people will never report the small failures and near misses that would allow you to learn and prepare for the future. When people are encouraged to speak up, especially on sensitive issues, leaders do a much better job of dealing with baffling conditions and taking good risks. In most hierarchies, especially at the top, leaders must work very hard to create the conditions for free exchange of ideas and real disagreement. Most leaders have an impact on the career success and financial rewards of those who work for them. In uncertain times people may speak up less, and the leader must work more to encourage it to happen.

Confronted and confounded by surprises, Winston Churchill said he used to ask himself the following four questions:

- Why didn't I know?
- Why didn't my people know?
- Why wasn't I told?
- What didn't I ask?

We suggest you ask yourself the same questions in order to encourage people to speak up. Does the culture you create as a leader encourage people to speak freely on any subject? Or are there likely to be repercussions for messengers who deliver bad news? Or for people who float provocative or contrary viewpoints?

Whole leaders have the courage to let people speak their minds, even if they disagree with their positions or philosophies. They also are sufficiently humble and open that others trust that they won't get cut off at the knees when they venture a contrary opinion. As a result, they have a firmer foundation to take risks despite the uncertainty—they have gathered a range of ideas and facts and can move forward with a broad base of knowledge before making a decision.

5. *Use your heart to understand and accept that anxiety underlies risk and uncertainty.*

Most people can live with uncertainty, but they will also feel anxiety about it. There is little a leader can do to remove or even reduce anxiety—it's a natural and healthy response to not knowing what the future will bring. Many leaders try to exhort followers out of their feelings—"let's control what we can control" or "there is no certainty in today's world!" are examples of things we've heard leaders say in an effort to be motivational. The reality is that anxiety can be acknowledged without becoming debilitating. Many people wonder whether a leader who does not feel—or at any rate does not show—any anxiety really understands the conditions facing the company. Good leaders walk a fine line, acknowledging people's experience while also moving them forward to take action.

6. *Use your head to analyze uncertainties and redefine them as opportunities through scenario planning.*

One recent study revealed that managers typically focus on only 55 percent of the actions that account for return on assets. A review of more than a hundred U.S. manufacturing firms with at least two strategic business units, in 160 industries, revealed that the other 45 percent of asset development came from external effects of general economic and political conditions and random events (35 percent), along with industry trends and developments (10 percent). These were areas where managers had not looked for opportunities because they believed that events were "beyond their control." However, redefining strategic opportunities that can flow from uncertainty is the last and most important step in redefining risk and opportunity.

Scenario planning has been used for years by companies wishing to explore the possibilities in a series of uncertain futures. It is different from contingency planning in that it does not limit thinking to one or two problems and try to prepare for them. Instead, scenario planning develops complex and comprehensive pictures of uncertain futures and then looks at possible opportunities as well as risks contained in each scenario. In the process it examines extreme pictures to gain insight into opportunities that might lie between the extremes. The overarching how-to theme is to recognize that opportunity exists in abundance when uncertainty flourishes. The demise of a company can be an opportunity for a leader to reinvent it. When brand risk looms, the changeability of the market might present leaders with a chance to reposition product lines in ways that will capitalize on emerging trends. Uncertainty is going to be with us for the foreseeable future, so there's not much point moaning about it or trying to find a risk-free harbor.

7. *Use your guts to examine your own risk profile and tolerance for risk and uncertainty.*

Don't make the mistake of thinking that visionary leaders such as Bill Weldon or Andrea Jung are so supremely confident that they never question or doubt themselves. In fact, it takes courage to question your assumptions. The easiest thing for leaders to do is operate out of their pet assumptions and use people around them to confirm the validity of what is assumed. Leaders with guts challenge themselves to determine if their implicit beliefs are viable, and they do that by talking continuously with people whose assumptions differ from theirs.

Andrea Jung led Avon's turnaround and displayed a great deal of guts in the process. Earlier we noted Jung had heart. But she exhibited courage, too, when she recognized that some of her assumptions were no longer relevant and she had to make changes. One of those changes was reducing the head count by 10 percent—a reduction of three thousand employees. Rather than delegate this task, she visited the places and people who were to be downsized and delivered the message herself. She took accountability and earned respect for her willingness to deliver bad news in person to the people most affected by her decision.

All of us have strengths and weaknesses when we approach risk and uncertainty. Many of these are related to our basic personality. In our book *Why CEOs Fail,* we examined eleven *derailers,* factors that cause leaders to lose the confidence of those around them when they deal with the stress of uncertainty and complexity. Each of these can create conditions in which appropriate risks may not be recognized, uncertainty may be miscalculated, or the wrong organizational culture may be developed for dealing with risk and uncertainty at an appropriate level.

WHOLE LEADERSHIP QUESTIONS TO
ASK YOURSELF ABOUT REDEFINING RISK AND UNCERTAINTY

If you embrace risk wholly, you stand a much better chance of seizing its inherent opportunities. Wrap your mind around the risk, feel its impact on yourself and on others, and use your bedrock beliefs to act on it.

Use Your Head
- What is the collective wisdom about the risk you're struggling with? Does this wisdom seem to be evolving in a certain direction?
- What are the key uncertainties in your business? How can you profit from them given your strengths?
- Have you engaged in scenario planning to stretch your mind regarding possible uncertainties for the future of your company?
- What might happen to make you more certain of what you should do? What are you looking for that would catalyze your willingness to take a chance and act?

Use Your Heart
- Do you understand why your employees may be reluctant to speak up about potential risks?
- Have you created a climate in which your people are willing to deliver bad news to you?
- Do you have any executives in place who do not set a climate where people will tell them bad news?
- Have you publicly recognized people who prevented future risks based on acknowledgment of past failures?

Use Your Guts
- Do you believe that leaders who are too conservative in regard to risk cannot grow their companies fast enough?
- Do you believe that being overly aggressive in terms of risk is only acceptable under stable, slow-moving conditions?
- Do you feel the best risks are the ones when you've done every possible analysis and you're reasonably assured of the outcome?
- Do you take risks by playing hunches, believing your instincts won't let you down?

Balance Conflicting Priorities

I N TODAY'S WORLD, COMPLEX PROBLEMS ARE DESCRIBED BY SOME urban planners as "wicked." A wicked problem has innumerable causes and cannot be definitely resolved. John Camillus notes five criteria for determining whether a problem is wicked. Briefly, it is wicked if it involves many stakeholders with conflicting priorities, its roots are tangled, it changes with every attempt to address it, you've never faced it before, and there's no way to evaluate whether a remedy will work. Sound familiar?

It seems like the more urgently leaders seek crystal balls, the cloudier the prospect becomes. At least that's how it seems to many CEOs and other senior executives who peer through mists of uncertainty and paradox to see what might happen. The harder they stare, the more the mists shift. Will oil prices go up or down? Will credit remain tight or loose? Will discretionary consumer spending increase, stay flat, or decrease? Is selling branded products or generics the answer for developing markets? Trying to figure out which emerging trend is significant and which will fade is frustrating. Leaders who bet wrong pay a significant price. Think used car lots filled with SUVs. Piles of CDs sold at garage sales. Brand new housing developments in the exurbs. Unpredictable uncertainty about a fast-changing, ever-expanding landscape always creates a haze, and it is not going to lift at any point soon.

Trying to predict the future with any precision is a fool's game; ignoring it is suicidal. Somewhere between prediction and neglect the right approach exists. Recent research has revealed a positive correlation between a leader's tolerance for ambiguity and the successful management of paradoxes. Debra Hunter says that a high tolerance for ambiguity entails a tendency to perceive ambiguous situations as desirable, whereas people with a low tolerance for ambiguity see ambiguous situations as threatening. Clearly, tolerance for ambiguity could help a leader cope with an increasingly uncertain world, but how do you develop it?

This is unfamiliar territory for head-only leaders who have relied for years on analytical tools to predict where markets and technologies are going and who see their responsibility as creating order out of chaos. Quick resolution of uncertain, ambiguous situations has always been the objective. It is called problem *solving,* and sometimes "decisive leadership." Unfortunately for head-only leaders, the world of senior leadership today more frequently calls for balancing paradoxes than for solving problems.

Uncertainty and ambiguity are also challenging for heart-only leaders who chart their course by listening and being open to a wide range of opinions. They become confused and many times are paralyzed by their desire to be responsive to everyone. Guts-only leaders are probably the most tolerant of ambiguity and uncertainty, but their danger is that they place too much faith in their instincts—which, if based on past experience, may be exactly wrong in a rapidly shifting environment.

We work with many scientists, chemists, engineers, and accountants. By training, they are usually able to absorb, digest, and analyze large amounts of information. Their challenge is in making the leap from information to implication. Frequently, head-only leaders will struggle with the implications because wild swings in social, economic, and technological trends undermine logical, fact-based forecasts. Guts-only leaders will miss the boat because their instincts don't function as well in an era where all the rules have changed and experience (which sharpens instinct) has become less relevant as a predictive tool. And heart-only leaders will have difficulty identifying future trends because they're drowning in a sea of opinions and feelings—the more they listen, the more open they are to fresh perspectives, and the more confused they become.

We're not dismissing the strengths of each type of partial leader. Far from it. What we are suggesting is that in an uncertain, interdependent world, leaders need to avail themselves of all three capabilities if they're going to avoid the obvious pitfall of overdoing their strengths.

THE WAY YOU SEE THE FUTURE DEPENDS ON YOUR VANTAGE POINT

Peter Koestenbaum, in his excellent book *Leadership,* notes, "Remember, it is not that we have so much to do that we cannot find time to think and act as leaders; on the contrary, it is because we do not think and act as leaders that we have so much to do." Balancing priorities of conflicting demands requires leaders to be clear about the issues and clear about how they balance their attention and their time. It requires them to "think and act as leaders."

The future impacts different leaders in different ways at different levels. If you're a line manager, for instance, you don't have to think too far into the future; your responsibilities are generally rooted in delivering results now. The more senior you become, however, the further out your time frame stretches. For senior leaders, looking ahead has become a much more difficult task than it used to be because the future is increasingly unpredictable, and because redirecting large bureaucracies is increasingly difficult in a less command-and-control world.

If you're a CEO, it's akin to playing roulette, but with only enough resources to place one bet on one spin of the wheel. Years ago, you could place a lot more bets on more spins. Plus, the game was often rigged—you had enough information to know what numbers were likely to come up. Now not only is everything riding on one spin, but the consequences of making the wrong bet can be catastrophic. Betting on the receipt of FDA approval, or the capacity of next-generation technology, or consumer response to a product are big choices with huge consequences. Observe the pharmaceutical, financial services, automobile, and newspaper industries. You might have to fire 25 percent of your organization or, worse, mortgage your company's long-term viability. These type of decisions are not limited to CEOs. Middle and senior managers are increasingly facing significant choices that can impact lots of people in large interdependent systems.

What really causes problems is after you make your bet: You choose a strategy or direction, and you're faced with the paradox of commitment. Like many senior leaders, your training and instinct is to look outward, determine what is likely to happen, and create a strategy designed to take advantage of or protect you from your "prediction." The problem? On one hand, you have been taught that leaders stay the course—they make a decision and stick with it. On the other hand, high degrees of uncertainty require course shifts—adaptability is the name of the game. This is the paradox of commitment, and it is the paradox of balancing conflicting priorities.

So what choice do you make? Do you change course and open yourself up to criticism that you're a waffler? As you well know, various communities tend to respond negatively when leaders say one thing and then admit they were wrong and move in another direction. More than one U.S. political leader has admitted making a mistake by supporting the Iraq war, saying that now, with fresh information, they are against it. While it would seem that this is an admirable quality—the ability to admit you're wrong and adapt as circumstances dictate—it is often perceived as the sign of a disingenuous or weak leader. People do not like leaders to appear wishy-washy or insincere in their beliefs.

Yet staying the course comes with its own negative repercussions. How long should you stay with a strategy as evidence piles up that it's not working? When do you accept that, despite your conviction that you were doing the right thing, changes in the environment have made your initial decision less than exact? Do you hang in there at all costs, hoping against hope that further events will eventually justify your decisions?

What all this boils down to is the following:

How to strike a balance between trying to predict an uncertain future and knowing you can't.

Although we all know that financial shocks are inevitable, who would have predicted a few years ago that after the stock market bubble of the nineties was pierced, it would be replaced by a housing bubble that would ultimately devastate the global financial system? Who would have predicted the global rise in commodity prices like wheat, corn, and rice, and the resultant impact on food prices worldwide? A few years ago, who would have thought that oil would top even $75, let alone $100 a barrel? Nonetheless, most of us could have seen the limited supply of fossil fuel and at least have been thinking about what it could mean for every organization, big or small. Most leaders

hope someone else is thinking about this for them, but almost everyone should have been concerned about this issue and planning for
contingencies. What happens if oil goes to $200? How will this
impact the supply chain of most organizations today? How will
it impact your customers? Your employees? Admittedly, you can't
predict these types of things with much accuracy. At the same time,
planning and developing a point of view, no matter where you sit
in the organization, is essential. It opens your eyes to new ideas,
helps you interact with a wider range of people, and can help you
take action in even the most unstable of times. And it allows you to
gain a better idea of how you should prioritize the allocation of your
resources and the attention of your organization.

HSN is a company whose leaders spend a large part of their time
planning for contingencies, because their customers are buying discretionary products with money not spent on gas, food, and other
essentials. The leadership team begins its meetings every week by asking, "What is happening that is affecting our business?" and "What
is happening that affects our employees, our customers, and our
future?" CEO Mindy Grossman believes that the discipline of regularly asking these questions and focusing on the uncertainty in the
environment results in the leaders' developing a point of view about
what they should address as a group.

The future has always been unpredictable. But there always
seemed to be short-term priorities and long-term priorities. You
knew you needed to pay attention to the short-term priorities and
that the long-term ones could "wait until later": until you had more
resources or until you had dealt with the current crisis. But now the
speed and scope of change means that the future may be here faster
than you think. As little as ten years ago—with less connectedness
through the Internet, less speed in how events unfolded, and less
competition—you might have missed an unpredictable future event
with fewer repercussions. Now change happens so fast and has such
a huge impact that taking your eye off the future for even a moment
can have serious consequences.

It used to be that concerns about significant potential events
in the future were confined to a relatively small list—you worried
about how the economy might affect your company, how stable your
suppliers were, how the marketplace might play itself out. But these
were finite events, and as unpredictable as they were, their impact

usually could be controlled. As discussed in Chapter Nine, you could have some time to use your resilience to return to normal operations. Now CEOs and senior leaders tell us that the degree of uncertainty has increased significantly because the rate of change has accelerated. You might have major litigation one week, followed by even more major litigation the next. Emerging market competitors might begin showing up in developed markets with cheaper products at acceptable quality at the same time regulatory pressure driven by politicians slows your own product pipeline. Events now come at CEOs and senior executives at a fast and furious clip, and the sheer speed of new and bewildering change can make even experienced leaders unsure about how to allocate their time and resources.

On top of that, the scale of these changes can shake entire industries. High oil prices create a boom market in corn (an ethanol ingredient), driving up commodity prices for almost all food manufacturers. High oil prices inspire increased online shopping, which disrupts traditional retailers. Excessive risks in lending to sub-prime borrowers and repackaging those loans can ultimately devastate big and small banks worldwide. When entire industries are rattled to their core, individual companies within those industries are thrown about like twigs in a hurricane.

So the uncertain future is no longer something you can deal with through annual strategic plans or with a problem-solution perspective. As noted in Chapter Nine, strategic risk management today requires a different mind-set. You have to pay attention and keep track of multiple variables. Global events that seem largely irrelevant need to be considered in a new light. Financial, consumer, political, and regulatory trends need to be discussed and debated for their potential impact. And rather than finding the right solution and moving on to the next opportunity, you have to balance your focus on many different issues simultaneously. That's asking a lot of any leader, and leaders respond to this challenge in both right and wrong ways.

BALANCING PRIORITIES OF ATTENTION

As noted in Chapter Nine, what you pay attention to determines what you do. If you do not track small failures or look closely at information on the competition or constantly scan the geopolitical environment, you may be caught dealing with a priority that seems urgent but is less important than the one you should be dealing with. Determining what you will pay attention to is your first choice in priority management and dealing with uncertainty. Here are three "don'ts" every leader should keep in mind when determining what to pay attention to.

Don't get caught facing the future with a purely internal focus.

Many managers can't escape the complex mechanisms of their own business. They don't take a good long look at the world outside their organizations because they're so enmeshed in the "fierce urgency of now"—their production problems, employment levels, business plan performance, or even their annual giving program. Most senior teams become consumed by these immediate issues, often believing the maxim, "If we don't address today, there will be no tomorrow." Yet now, the uncertainty and potential impact of the future demand reallocation of attention because disruptions in the environment can disrupt business models with lightning speed. Uncertain markets, competitors, new technologies, and the like can only be anticipated and managed by routinely tracking them, even if they don't have any immediate impact on your business. Senior leaders must now spend some of their time reading, listening, and thinking about the external environment. Senior teams must now allocate precious meeting time to looking out rather than in. Jim Collins has described "Level 5 leaders," the highest performers, as always looking out the window to identify where success comes from and looking in the mirror to find the source of failure. This trait of top leaders is especially valuable when dealing with an uncertain future.

Don't fail to challenge your assumptions.

Forgive us for repeating ourselves, but leaders often don't challenge their beliefs when it comes to dealing with uncertainty. They assume that people will always buy music in stores. They assume that their organization will always work best with a decentralized structure because local management demands it. They assume that Europe will continue to be the most important foreign market because that is where the resources and infrastructure are invested today. These could be right or wrong assumptions, but for every business and every individual industry, whatever is assumed based on the past is likely to be wrong for the future. As comfortable as it is to determine your priorities based on your past experience—and as much as it saves time and money—it is today a deadly practice.

Don't allow arrogance to creep into your view of the future.

By definition, arrogance makes you vulnerable to surprises. When you convince yourself that you have the answer—that you have a winning formula that will triumph in all circumstances—then something in the future is bound to get you. As Murphy's Law postulates, "If something can go wrong, it will go wrong." Andy Grove, former chairman of Intel and author of *Only the Paranoid Survive,* suggests that "sooner or later, something fundamental in your business world will change." The future humbles us all. Senior teams may be especially vulnerable to the temptation to believe that, like Yertle the Turtle, because they sit on top of the organization, they command all that they see, including the future. The challenge for everyone is to look into an uncertain future with a learner's mind-set and maintain flexibility.

You're especially likely to make these mistakes if you're a partial leader. When confronting some element of the future that is volatile and unpredictable, you reflexively fall back on your singular strength. If you're a head type, you try and assemble data to justify your decision, no matter how concerned you might be that it's wrong. If you're a heart type, you gather people around you and talk yourself out of what you fear about the future, taking comfort in the fact that at least some people agree with your direction. If you're a guts type, you take action to brush aside the hesitation, creating a false sense of certainty about the outcome of your actions.

Fear of the future also tempts whole leaders to rely on whatever their dominant capability is. But their more balanced approach gives them access to other capabilities. They possess the option and the opportunity to try something different.

BALANCING PRIORITIES OF CHOICE

Once you believe that you have an adequate balance between external and internal focus, that you are challenging your assumptions about your past success, and that you are humble enough not to be caught up in the hubris of market leadership, you must face the uncertainty of what choices to make about an uncertain future. Balancing the priorities of choice begins with an understanding of problems as opposed to paradoxes.

Very simply, a *problem can be solved* so you can move on. Raise revenues, cut costs, ensure enough leadership talent for the future of your organization—all problems to be solved. Paradoxes, by contrast, cannot be solved: they have to be balanced. If I raise revenues, I may add costs—but I need to cut costs—and I need to raise revenues. I need to pay attention to both, and balance both simultaneously, and the balancing act will never end.

Paradoxes mean balancing equally important but contradictory priorities. This is very different from lining up a string of problem priorities and solving them once and for all. As discussed in Chapter Eight, on stakeholders, the higher you go in an organization, the more you are balancing the priorities of divergent strategies and the conflicting demands of stakeholders, and the less you are solving the operational problems of the business.

Here's how whole leaders address the task of balancing conflicting choices.

WHOLE LEADERSHIP APPROACH TO BALANCING CONFLICTING PRIORITIES

Amy Woods Brinkley, a senior executive with the Bank of America who has spent thirty years in a wide range of roles, including chief risk officer, believes that what is needed is "unambiguous leadership in ambiguous times." Brinkley has told us that she believes the best leaders combine principles that they deeply believe in with an appreciation and tolerance for the management of paradoxes.

Grappling with decisions when things are in a state of flux and the unexpected keeps happening has driven more than one leader into retirement—or into consulting. It's enormously difficult to take action when it seems as if events will conspire to prove any action wrong. And it's just as difficult to do nothing since an uncertain future gives rise to great opportunities that demand action.

Whole leadership provides an alternative to being stuck in this conundrum. Or rather, it allows you to think about your options in broader terms than "either/or." Consider taking the actions listed in Figure 10.1 when facing a black-or-white decision about the future.

A classic paradox that all managers have to deal with is that between performance and people. Russ Eisenstat and his colleagues have come to the conclusion that leaders who are successful in balancing contradictory demands—focusing on the needs of the shareholder *and* the need to motivate and inspire employees—combine openness with the "unvarnished truth" while at the same time delivering short-term financial performance by focusing employees on the core mission and values of the organization.

1. *Use your head to clarify your long-term vision and values for the organization.*

Here's the typical scenario. You make a critical decision, and as the weeks and months pass, you second-guess yourself. The more people you talk to, the more you start worrying that you've taken the wrong course of action. When you go back and analyze the logic of your decision, however, it still seems valid; you can rationalize the

FIGURE 10.1. *Balancing Conflicting Priorities.*

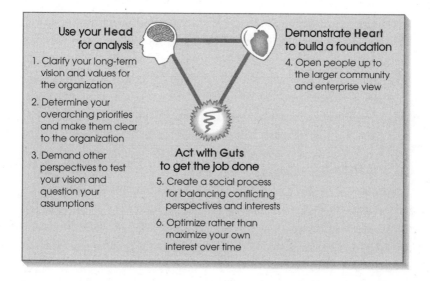

setbacks that make others doubt what you're doing. Your head tells you to stay the course. However, your heart says listen to what others are telling you, and you want to make a shift.

When your head and heart cancel each other out and there's no way to know for certain what to do, rely on your vision for the future. What is your point of view about the future? As a leader you will need to have a clear position from which you lead. This can be an organizational mission, a vision, or a set of values, but you cannot lead successfully in times of uncertainty and turmoil without some fundamental guiding principles around which you organize your choices. For large companies such as Johnson & Johnson this can be a corporate credo that guides individual managers in making daily decisions. For small companies this can be the overriding purpose: why they were created and why they exist. For individual leaders, this can be a clear vision combined with a clear sense of purpose, or why they get up every morning to serve in this organization. We have seen leaders who do not have this clear vision and purpose, and it not only makes them ineffective leaders in times of uncertainty, it also creates personal agony as they wrestle with what choices to do next.

2. *Use your head to determine your overarching priorities and make them clear to the organization.*

Most leaders stumble when they translate a clear vision and values into even clearer priorities. Good leaders communicate over and over the key success factors around which the vision will be measured. For companies this means "overarching priorities" such as winning in a particular market, or focusing on emerging markets, or something that sets out the plan of action. Poor leaders take the priorities a step further, telling people what they should be doing rather than encouraging them to figure it out based on the established priorities.

3. *Use your head to demand other perspectives to test your vision and question your assumptions.*

You may recall children's magazines that offer visual puzzles that ask you to find pictures of common objects hidden amid detailed illustrations. At first glance, these objects are invisible. Sometimes, it takes turning the page and looking at the illustration from a fresh angle or covering up part of the puzzle to focus your attention until the hidden objects materialize.

Staring into the future, it's easy to overlook the hidden objects in your own picture. Visualizing them requires a shift in perspective or change in focus. Chaos theory is a way of looking at organizations as whole systems, encouraging you to detect patterns in seemingly random events. Meg Wheatley has said, "In chaos theory, it is true that you can never tell where the system is headed until you've observed it over time. Order emerges, but it doesn't emerge instantly." Bill Weldon of Johnson & Johnson has said that a leader must be able to endure chaos and demands for clarity until the right course of action emerges, around which an organization coalesces. Our colleague Ron Heifetz has written about achieving a "balcony perspective," as a way of "stepping back in the midst of action and asking, 'What's really going on here?'" Heifetz believes that the work of leaders is to regulate the pressure of chaos and uncertainty so people will work together to solve problems and not delegate them upward to their leader.

What we are suggesting is that no matter how uncertain the future may appear, you may be able to discern useful patterns if you change the way you look at things. For us, whole leadership provides a new lens for observing an uncertain future. Instead of looking at things from your traditional head or heart or guts perspective, you can broaden your vision. In this way, you may "feel" a development that your analytical side doesn't reveal or you may see something on the horizon that doesn't fit with your traditional view of the world.

If you recall, Apple and Steve Jobs launched iTunes at a time when the music industry was in chaos—file sharing was eating into profits, record companies were being criticized for pricing CDs too high, and intellectual property rights were being challenged with lawsuits and countersuits. It was widely assumed that file-sharing customers would be loath to pay money to download music. Apple and Jobs, however, took a step back, observed the future, and saw something no one else saw—that users really wanted convenience and choice, and in return would obey the law.

New, different, and important perspectives may be represented by people in your organization who are seen as contrarian or eccentric. The perspectives may be discovered in a competitor's view of the marketplace that does not match your own, or the view of an academic who has researched a strategic concern of your organization and has discovered your assumptions about the future are faulty or your information is inadequate in scale and scope. Of greatest value, however, may be the perspective of your own employees who are on the front line with customers, look at things through a generational perspective, or are just too new to the company to have embodied the traditional way of seeing things.

Whole leaders demand these perspectives. They are not content with making the world simple and easy. They know it is complex and uncertain, and when things are obvious, they know they may be wrong. This is not second-guessing; it is strong leadership.

4. *Use your heart to open people up to the larger enterprise view.*

Much as your vision requires your head, your heart connects you to your people and helps people connect with each other. The enterprise view that good leaders creatively convey in many different ways comes down to "we're all in this together." This sense of community and engagement pulls people together and helps them focus on serving, growing, and winning as a whole organization rather than beating the people in the next set of cubicles or the function down the hall.

5. *Use your guts to create a social process for balancing conflicting perspectives and interests.*

Difficult problems cannot be solved through traditional head analysis. Instead, social processes must be designed to engage stake-holders, explore related issues, reevaluate a problem's definition, and reconsider traditional assumptions.

The key here is social process. The world is filled with paradoxes and conflicting demands. The CEO's world requires constant trade-offs and balancing of one good against another. It is not a matter of choosing between right and wrong, but between two rights—that is what is maddening and what makes every decision in a complex world more uncertain with regard to its positive impact and the price to be paid with other interest groups and constituencies whose concerns will have to be ignored to make any decision with limited resources. Someone wins and someone loses almost all the time. Even though both/and thinking can allow everyone to be satisfied over the long run, individual decisions will favor one constituency over another.

As we noted earlier, when two conflicting interests are equally true and valid, you have encountered a paradox, and paradoxes cannot be solved, only managed. They also require that both sides acknowledge the legitimacy of the other perspective, while at the same time neither agreeing with what the other side wants nor denying it every time. Lack of willingness to acknowledge the legitimacy of another's perspective is the reason why certain conflicts continue unmanaged and unresolved, such as the ones between the Palestinians and the Israelis, the Indians and the Pakistanis, or to a lesser extent, the Democrats and the Republicans.

In companies similar conflicts are represented by competing functions or regions that are unable to adopt an enterprise perspective. Conflicting priorities in an organization are usually endemic and involve paradoxes that must be managed over time. Global franchise requirements versus local market needs is typical of a paradox that must be managed rather than solved. Innovation requires that a process must be established for conflicting interests to present their viewpoint for a negotiated settlement to be made on differing portions of the problem.

The Swedish manufacturer Ericsson has established quarterly forums to bring together country managers and business leaders to examine the conflicting needs of local customers and global business priorities to ensure that the tough choices of resource allocation balance global and local priorities. This provides a formal opportunity for the company to deal with a conflict of priorities that it knows will never end. Rather than allowing these conflicts to be fought out in internecine warfare, its leaders surfaced the clash and institutionalized a way to manage it. This strategy is key to managing the conflicting priorities of a global organization.

We frequently use the Competing Values framework developed by Jeff DeGraff to help senior leaders understand that the different perspectives shaped by people's underlying values can be harnessed to drive innovation rather than stymie progress. DeGraff assigns a color to each perspective, with "yellows" valuing collaboration, "reds" valuing control, "blues" emphasizing competing, and "greens" emphasizing creativity. Each of these approaches plays out differently in the process of innovation and problem solving, and by understanding and appreciating the strengths of the values of each one, you can learn to use rather than resist the contributions of others.

6. *Use your guts to optimize rather than maximize your own interests over time.*

This brings us to the most difficult aspect of balancing priorities. In the long run, to balance two conflicting positions of equal importance, one must commit to not winning every confrontation. Since the other position is equally valid and in need of attention, you must determine which battles you have to win and which ones you are prepared to lose. In other words, you must seek to optimize rather than maximize your self-interests over time, acknowledging that the legitimacy of the other side's needs requires you to meet their demands in some consistent way for the sake of the enterprise as a whole.

This clearly is a guts issue. Leaders are often caught between the need to maintain an ongoing relationship with other people or interests in the organization while at the same time representing the interests of their own function, region, or team. This is the dilemma of every negotiator or representative, and often impedes senior teams. The interpersonal and diplomatic skills needed for problem solving must be backed up with the courage to balance conflicting demands and make short-term sacrifices for larger, longer-term objectives. Only whole leaders can successfully balance and communicate these decisions in complex and uncertain situations.

WHOLE LEADERSHIP QUESTIONS TO ASK YOURSELF ABOUT BALANCING PRIORITIES

Use Your Head

- Are you making a continuous effort to balance your attention and lift your focus from your business's internal issues to see trends and events that may have nothing to do with your immediate problems, but may have a lot to do with what you're going to be facing in a year or two?
- Do you attempt to find patterns in what appear to be chaos and random events by taking a step back?
- Do you understand which paradoxes are most important to manage on a continuing basis, and have you put in place mechanisms for balancing the conflicting demands of right versus right?

Use Your Heart

- Are you using external resources—academics, consultants, and others—to provide analyses that test your assumptions and your strategies?
- Do you have a way of testing your vision and values with various constituencies in your organization?
- Do you deliberately reach out to those in your organization who disagree with you to better understand their concerns and perspectives as a way of testing your own views?

Use Your Guts

- Do you rely on your vision and values to steer you through uncertainty? If your analysis tells you one thing about the future and the reactions of other people tell you something else, how do you resolve this conflict?
- Do you put the company first when you realize that the interest of your organizational unit may need to be sacrificed this time to achieve overall company objectives?
- Have you found ways to manage the difficult paradox of maintaining your credibility as a leader with your people and a trusted colleague in leading the enterprise as a whole?

CHAPTER 11

Be Clear What You Have the Courage to Stand For

T HE JUNGIAN ANALYST JAMES HOLLIS ONCE OBSERVED, "WE CAN spend decades climbing the ladder—only to realize too late that we have placed it against the wrong wall." Getting clear about what you believe in and what drives you has many benefits—from putting the purpose of your life in perspective to helping you endure one more boring and seemingly never-ending meeting. Useful as it is to define your leadership vision, values, and purpose, getting clear about values is sometimes a counterintuitive challenge for bright, successful leaders. For years, they've relied on their knowledge or experience to get them through tough situations. By being the smartest person in the room, they've given their people the insights necessary to solve problems. By using their extensive knowledge of a given field, they've strategized their way into opportunities.

But relying on what they believe in? We often begin global executive development programs by asking leaders to react to the following quote:

"The more complex, diverse, and uncertain the world becomes, the more leaders are faced with choosing between the right and right of conflicting constituencies. The more this occurs, the deeper leaders must go inside themselves to determine who they are, what they are trying to accomplish, and what they will have the courage to be known for."

We ask leaders to confront these questions: What, exactly, do you believe? How do you describe your core purpose to yourself and others? When the chips are down and the pressure is up, who shows up?

Ralph Shrader, chairman and CEO of Booz Allen Hamilton, maintains that the fundamentals of leadership in a "liquid world" are based on solid personal principles. He advocates accepting change and uncertainty, being willing to consider all points of view, but—most of all—developing a "calm center" that allows you to maintain clarity. Of course, this is exactly what is needed when you're leading in a perfect storm.

Even in a perfect storm, you'll encounter simple situations and decisions that don't require a clarified vision or belief system; you can just make a choice the way you always have. As situations become more complex and chaotic, however, your personal clarity of vision and courage become much more central to your response. For complex situations in which no right answers exist, many competing ideas vie for your attention, and unpredictability is the norm, you must engage people in dialogue and provide guidance on parameters based on your vision and values. Chaotic situations full of turbulence and tension confront you with too many decisions and leave you no time to think. To lead effectively in this environment, you must operate from your deepest sense of values and your gut instinct. In a very real sense, you're providing clear direction from your deepest sense of who you are, what you are trying to achieve, and what you have the courage to be known for.

This is serious stuff. It requires a combination of strength and flexibility. The payoff is the ability to lead with greater purpose and passion. Leaders who act authentically can afford to be transparent, and transparency inspires and motivates people. More than that, it provides guidance in a chaotic environment. This is an opportunity to find what Bill George refers to as your "True North." George, the former chairman and CEO of Medtronic, believes that a leader's Truth North, like a compass needle, points toward a magnetic pole that is the purpose of their leadership. He maintains that when leaders discover their real passion and purpose, they will be authentic in a way that naturally draws people to them.

In turbulent times, leaders often lose their way. Ironically, these chaotic environments are when it's most important to know what you stand for. A guiding vision is essential in the midst of uncertainty and complexity, since analysis alone doesn't yield answers. We work with many senior leaders on finding their purpose and reflecting on what motivates them. Sometimes this requires reflection and understanding the life events that have shaped a leader's philosophy and sense of purpose. In an earlier book, we described how life events as well as career events constitute "leadership passages," creating a crucible of learning and self-insight. Events such as death of a loved one, divorce, moving into general management, or living in another country are among the range of experiences that shape leaders. These passages facilitate an understanding of your own vision and values and can ground you in times of uncertainty.

Partial Leaders and Beliefs

As crucial as vision and values are, they're not the whole story. You've probably encountered leaders who were zealous in their beliefs about how their companies should operate but, being partial leaders, they were still doomed to fail. Their inflexibility, inability to connect with a diverse group of people, lack of analytical insight, or simple-minded approaches to complex issues led the company off a cliff. Enron comes to mind. Despite their fervent beliefs, Enron executives alienated key people and implemented flawed strategies. Even though they made a convincing case for why they were doing what they were doing, they were operating with only part of their full leadership capabilities.

Authenticity is attributed to you by others rather than created by you. Leaders and followers both associate authenticity with sincerity, honesty, and integrity. Being genuine is something you can control, but being authentic is the perception others have of you. This is not just semantics. If you try to convince others you're an authentic leader, you'll fail. You need to have this quality validated by others.

To accord the judgment of full authenticity, people need to see alignment between your beliefs and your head, heart, and guts. They want to see someone who has a strong reality orientation, is sensitive to the needs of others, and has the self-discipline and courage that turns vision and values into true authenticity.

A Whole Leadership Approach to Being Clear About What You Have the Courage to Be Known For

Fortunately, many leaders are more naturally values-driven today than in the past. This is due in part to how our model of effective leadership has evolved. Until relatively recently, a leader's watchwords were loyalty and obedience: expect the former and demand the latter. In turn, a leader was loyal and obedient to the next boss up the line. The leader's own beliefs were subsumed by the larger organizational needs. A company's policies and processes, structure and strategy dictated those beliefs.

Today, however, the complexity and uncertainty of most organizations and markets leave leaders no place to hide. The simple loyalty-and-obedience formula of the past is blown away when they encounter multiple bosses in a matrix organization or the churn of downsizing and offshoring of jobs. Leaders today must look inside themselves and understand who they are, what they are trying to accomplish, and what they will have the courage to be known for. Figure 11.1 outlines how you can meet this challenge.

1. *Use your heart to develop an awareness of what you truly value.*

After 9/11 many people discovered that they had not really focused on what they truly valued in life—until they saw other businesspeople die in a flash and realized they were just as vulnerable. In executive programs, we ask leaders to reflect on questions developed

FIGURE 11.1. *Be Clear What You Have the Courage to Stand For.*

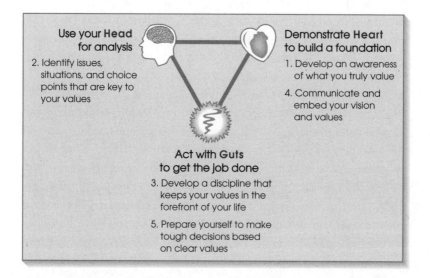

Use your **Head** for analysis

2. Identify issues, situations, and choice points that are key to your values

Demonstrate **Heart** to build a foundation

1. Develop an awareness of what you truly value

4. Communicate and embed your vision and values

Act with **Guts** to get the job done

3. Develop a discipline that keeps your values in the forefront of your life

5. Prepare yourself to make tough decisions based on clear values

by our friend Kevin Cashman, like "what is the meaning of life and how does it inform your role as a leader?" Or "what is truth and how does it relate to your leadership?"

The reaction is very interesting—of fifty managers in a room, some can immediately launch into a discussion of their feelings about these issues with little effort, because this is a level on which they live. But a number always find the exercise frightening; they have never thought about questions like these, and they are struck with how little they have reflected on what they truly value and what it might mean to their leadership style and philosophy.

Some leaders truly love to get up in the morning and turn a profit. They are driven by the numbers, the competition, and the chance to improve margins and return on investment for shareholders. It is their life's passion. While this is supposed to be the passion of every business leader, most business leaders we have worked with do not get up in the morning driven by this vision. Most get up to fulfill some other dream—serving customers better, growing their employees, making life better for people throughout the world. When these accomplishments can be matched with profitable activities, they are completely fulfilled. If not, some may seek fulfillment somewhere else.

Be clear about what you truly value—and when possible match that with your leadership role. Reframe the work you do to restate it at a higher level. Find your purpose in returning value to shareholders, winning in the marketplace, and sustaining growth. Drivers vary, but you should try to build a case that aligns your passion with your responsibilities—it will serve you well as you work your way through an uncertain world.

2. *Use your head to identify issues, situations, and choice points that are key to your values.*

An uncertain future demands leaders who are aware of their values and can use them to guide their actions when choice points arrive and data are conflicting, overwhelming, or confusing, or there are little or no data on which to draw conclusions. In other words, they make values-based judgments. Being able to do so begins with a clear understanding of your values and aspirations and clarity about what you are trying to accomplish.

After Bill Ford became CEO of Ford Motor Company at a relatively young age, he focused on making the company Green. His environmental emphasis came before the movement had really picked up steam, and he encouraged Ford to bring to market a number of hybrid vehicles. But a variety of other issues caused Ford to lose market share, endure labor issues, and otherwise not perform, and it became clear to Bill Ford that he was not the best person to lead the company into the future. While he represented a strong commitment to the environment and distinguished himself as the "greenest" chief executive in the auto industry, other issues confronting the Ford Motor Company overwhelmed him. He stepped aside so the company could bring in Alan Mulally of Boeing, who could better serve the company's need to survive and succeed during tough times.

Bill Ford is a good example of someone who discovered a conflict between his personal purpose and his responsibilities. He considered his true dedication to the company, the brand, his extended family, and the causes in which he believed, and he realized that he was not the best person to lead in Ford's current situation. Sometimes, like Bill Ford, you are forced to make a choice. If you choose not to follow your vision and values you may keep your job, but you may lose your authenticity. In that case, you may also lose your leadership and not be as successful. As Stephen R. Covey has noted, lining up your "compass" (your values and passions) with your "clock" (your roles, responsibilities, and activities) is critical to leading yourself and others.

Many people focus on the match between their values and their career as they experience the choice points of what field to enter, what company to work for, and what mentor or boss to follow. These are important times to reflect not only on the excitement of the opportunity being offered but also on your deepest aspirations. It is not easy to turn down a wonderful job with great benefits in an organization that's engaged in an activity that conflicts with your values or principles. But it is harder to find yourself in an organization or a job that you do not respect because of the underlying values and objectives on which the organization operates. Most people join organizations and leave supervisors. Make sure to have as much alignment as possible between you, your supervisor, and your organization's vision and values, and if you can't, decide to endure the dissonance or take action to resolve it.

3. *Use your guts to develop a discipline that keeps your values in the forefront of your life.*

Keeping your values front and center requires discipline. If you don't take time out to reflect periodically, you'll get caught up in the grind. The daily complexity, diversity, and uncertainty will distract you from your beliefs. When you're racing against deadlines and dealing with unpredictable people and events, there's little time to figure out what you believe in and how to act on this belief. Ron Heifetz recommends having a "sanctuary," a place for reflection or removing yourself from the action, where you can achieve new insight. Without a sanctuary, you are vulnerable to insistent bosses, organizational policies, and rationalization. If you aren't regularly thinking about what your beliefs are, then you'll be subject to other people's beliefs. Finding this sanctuary requires consistent, conscious effort. Many leaders tell themselves they need to step back and think about things, but they make only token efforts to do so.

Designate a place and a regular time to visit that place. It doesn't matter whether it's an empty office or a clearing in the woods near your office, or if it's regular morning meditation, weekly reflection, or journaling. Find a way to keep your purpose and values front and center in your life or they will fade away to a distant second that you will have trouble calling up when you need them. As long as you have this retreat that you can regularly return to, then you'll have the opportunity to make your values part of your instinctive reaction to life's events.

This kind of clarity gives you resilience in the face of disappointment and enables you to bring your organization back to focus on its primary purpose and vision. We spoke earlier about the importance of resilience in organizations that are recovering from unexpected crises. As you would probably guess, the degree to which organizations recover quickly from a crisis in large part depends on the degree to which their leaders can recover. Leaders who keep their core vision and values front and center in their lives have them when they need them to recover from unexpected personal and organizational shocks.

4. *Use your heart to communicate and embed your vision and values in your organization.*

The best leaders are explicit about their vision and values. People in the company know what they stand for and they put their stamp on the organization.

Nobody was unclear what Walt Disney saw as his vision for the Disney organization—it was to bring generations of families together in an activity that would reinforce family relationships and family values. To achieve this, he invented the theme park that would be fun for parents as well as children. And then he anticipated their every need—from food to strollers for babies to guides and umbrellas—to make their experience as effortless as possible so they could concentrate on one another and the fun they were having together.

Have a clear vision and values, communicate them, and when possible embed them into the fabric of the organization. Use your values to guide the annual planning process, and to provide choice points for investments and employees and customer relations. Make sure your people can demonstrate how these values affect their decisions and their actions. That only happens with leaders who are conscious of their values and make them explicit to others.

Ultimately a leader's vision and values should also be reflected in the company's brand in the marketplace. If a brand is already established from a past leader, then any leader in an organization must be sure to be able to live that brand, reinforce it, and develop it. Great brands stand for great values. They not only represent an aspirational vision that people can identify with, they deliver a promise to consumers and other stakeholders that is seen as valuable and important. A true leader not only has a clear vision and values but has communicated it, embedded it, and translated it into the marketplace in a way that provides clear choices in an uncertain world.

5. *Use your guts to prepare yourself to make tough decisions based on clear values.*

Bill Ford faced a choice point between his concern for the company and his personal status and he chose the company. In the process he made a statement of his values—the company was more important than he was, even though his name was on the door and even though his concern for the environment will in the long run prove as important to the auto industry as the success of the company, or more so.

Today, enlightened leaders expect to be challenged. They want their people to speak up. Notions such as empowerment, participatory decision making, and matrixes have evolved the model. When you can't expect blind loyalty and demand obedience, you need an alternative leadership philosophy. Relying on your own beliefs has become central to this philosophy. When you don't know if a merger might happen tomorrow, if your key people might leave and join a competitor, if your CEO might downsize a quarter of the workforce, if you will manage to make sense of a rapidly changing global marketplace, if you will be able to motivate people who come from backgrounds very different from your own . . . then all you have left is being clear about your own truths.

Leaders many times become clear about their values when they've been through a crucible experience. This type of experience can run the gamut: opening an office in a country where you feel like a foreigner literally and figuratively, being fired from a job you love, or finding your place in a downsized, restructured organization.

A crucible presents you with tough obstacles. It shakes your sense of yourself and your worldview. It causes you to take a step back, reflect, and rethink your assumptions. It requires you to assess your options. It may involve failure from which you have to rebound.

Most of all, it tests your character.

While you can't necessarily schedule crucible experiences—nor would most people want to—you can open yourself to them. Gravitate toward stretch jobs and risk-taking opportunities. Be willing to try something new, even if it entails a certain amount of risk. As a result, you'll be more likely to find yourself in a crucible than your colleagues who choose safe, secure paths.

Crucibles are defining moments, and they help you come to terms with what you really believe. There's the old saying: What doesn't kill you makes you stronger. We can usually spot leaders who have been through some sort of crucible in their lives, since they project strength of character that others lack. The moment you meet them, you understand that they operate from a place of deep values and centered calm in the perfect storm.

WHOLE LEADERSHIP QUESTIONS TO ASK YOURSELF ABOUT WHAT YOU HAVE THE COURAGE TO BE KNOWN FOR

Stephen R. Covey has noted that "Until you have done the inside-out work on yourself, you will not solve the fundamental problems of your organization, nor will you be able to truly empower others." To become the type of leader who operates from a position of beliefs and values, ask yourself the following questions:

Use Your Head
• Are you aware of what you believe in that makes a difference in how you lead your organization? Are there values that define what you believe are the right and wrong things to do in a position of leadership?

- Do you have a physical space to which you can retreat and give yourself peace and quiet in which to reflect on these beliefs?
- Are you able to maintain awareness of your beliefs amid a chaotic business environment, and can you use your awareness to determine when it's appropriate to make a stand based on these beliefs and when it's not?

Use Your Heart

- When do you feel really alive and excited about what you are doing? How often does this happen at work?
- Do the people around you know what's important to you as a leader? Can they see what's important through observing your actions and behaviors?
- Do you see leadership as a team sport? To what degree do you find yourself making decisions in isolation rather than working with others to ensure that you do not wander off in the wrong direction?

Use Your Guts

- Have you ever been through a crucible-like situation, either in your career or in your personal life? What impact did it have on you?
- What type of adversity have you faced and what obstacles did you need to overcome? What did you learn about yourself? How did it help you define who you are and what you value?
- Are you vigilant against lapsing into a dogmatic position? Are you sufficiently flexible to adapt and adjust as situations change? Do you rely on your beliefs but also examine them regularly?

PART
THREE

Developing Whole Leaders and Teams

CHAPTER 12

Aligning Your Company's Talent to Navigate the Storm

MOST LARGE GLOBAL COMPANIES HAVE IDENTIFIED "TALENT" as their key business strategy. Boards and CEOs are now directly involved in reviewing their company's leadership pipeline. HR executives are defining future leadership requirements given corporate growth projections and the supply and readiness of their leaders. The result? Many are worried about both talent and leadership, because they see the looming retirement of Baby Boomers and a compression in their leadership pipeline to groups of leaders at approximately the same age or stage of their development. Even more significantly, however, they're worried that a large number of their leaders are simply unprepared to handle the future's promise of even greater complexity, diversity, and uncertainty.

Many companies try to prop up their pipeline by defining the "competencies" that will constitute good leadership. A corporate leadership model can be very useful, especially when it is tied to the leadership needs of future strategic growth. We have encountered many of these models and find that they often describe a broad range of attitudes, behaviors, and skills. While useful as definitions of needed leadership talent, such models usually have too many competencies (we have seen over seventy-five) and most leaders cannot even remember them, let alone act on them. More disturbingly, these models are then used for performance reviews, making reviewing a herculean task and judging people on factors they couldn't possibly practice.

To be fair, most companies have found that the only way to deal with competency-based models is to focus on those few behaviors most needed for the next business cycle. Growth, globalization, innovation, cost containment, or other strategic initiatives will allow a prioritization that enables specific managers to focus on those skills they most need to develop.

But some companies are astute enough to grasp that a simpler leadership model can also be useful in a complex environment. Colgate, Burberry, and Johnson & Johnson have all adopted one form or another of our "whole leadership" or head, heart, and guts model. Rather than trying to map all the leadership skills complexity might demand, these companies are using head, heart, and guts as a metaframework within which to place the needed competences of their managers.

ENTERPRISE LEADERSHIP: A LARGER FOCUS

In global companies, there is renewed emphasis on "enterprise leadership." These large, complex, and interdependent corporations have mostly functional career paths, but require general managers who can manage all functions well. While this has always been the challenge for managers moving from functional to general management, the new complexity and uncertainty has made the transition even more difficult. Consider for a moment the management requirements when technologies such as file sharing are converging with telephony. How can you get scientists, engineers, marketers, and designers to all work together on the next generation of cell phones? Or another challenge—if a company wants to grow in emerging markets, how do you get different business units to collaborate in those markets to capitalize on joint investments, brand, and talent—rather than encouraging each business unit to focus only on its own objectives?

To develop enterprise leaders, many companies transfer people across business units, or functions, or send them abroad to experience living and working in a different culture. We have found that companies are much more intentional and disciplined about moving relatively new leaders than they used to be. They have also used high-potential action learning programs to provide young profession-als with unique experiences on cross-functional teams that examine enterprise-wide issues. The ultimate goal is the development of gen-eral managers with an enterprise view. These actions are effective, but they take time, often ten or more years to produce general managers with sufficient depth and range of experience.

We have found that experienced general managers today are still primarily focused on their own business unit, rather than the whole company. In response, companies often tinker with the reward system, including shifting the percentage allocated to corporate as opposed to business unit performance. While this is useful and many times necessary, we have found that most leaders don't get up every day and decide what to do based on the percentage of their pay devoted to a particular unit's performance. At senior levels, pay is rarely a motiva-tor. It can be a demotivator if seen as inadequate, but most senior lead-ers are more challenged by winning, growing a business, or advancing and gaining recognition in their careers. The same is true for most people—as discussed in Chapter Seven, meaning, however defined, can be more important than money in light of a total career.

To make enterprise leadership a focal point for leaders, companies must develop their people and their culture from both explicit and implicit perspectives. Explicitly, they must create a simple, clear pic-ture of successful enterprise leaders who feel accountable for the entire company as well as their own businesses. And they must create implicit cultural practices that support the explicit expectations—rather than undermining them, as often happens in organizations today.

We recently asked fifty top leaders of a major bank to write down on a card—without giving their names—one "rule of the road" they could not violate if they wanted to continue working in the bank. We then read all the cards to the group, sometimes to spontaneous laugh-ter and applause. "Never disagree with your boss in a public meeting" was the most common rule. "Make sure your revenue forecasts are at least 20 percent below what you know you can actually deliver so you will emerge as a hero at bonus time" or "walk the square by talking to every other business unit leader before presenting in a meeting," and "make sure your own results are in the bag before agreeing to help another business." The anonymity of the exercise allowed them to uncover some important truths.

These unwritten truths constitute the implicit leadership model of the company, and every company has them. An important question is whether the implicit model is functional or dysfunctional—that is, does it enable achieving business results and executing the company strategy, or impede it? And more important, what does successful leadership look like? We usually start with the executive team and the CEO, sometimes initiating a real debate about motivation, leadership, and accountability.

These are the types of discussions integral to whole leadership development. Without them, you're only developing part of the individual for part of the organization. During a perfect storm, such development is insufficient. For talent to be maximized, companies must have the guts to tackle these tough, implicit truths, the heart to deal with the people issues involved, and the head to grasp the implications for both leaders and the larger organization.

BUILDING A TALENT STRATEGY

Most organizations have a talent philosophy that has evolved beyond the "cream rises to the top" and "cash is king" notions of the past. While they recognize that compensation is important, they grasp that it's not the only thing. Although they try to engineer their compensation systems to produce the leadership behavior they think is needed, they usually complement their compensation-based incentives with a process designed to attract, train, develop, and identify high potentials. To orchestrate this process, they assign an individual (usually from HR) to create a talent strategy.

These talent strategies often do a good job of *efficiently* moving people into current leadership roles, helping to identify, train, and develop individuals who are best matched for different business or functional needs. Efficiency, however, is not enough during an era of swirling change and head-spinning surprise. It merely ensures that managers possess the right subject expertise and experience plus the identified leadership skills for the job. The specified skills, unfortunately, tend to be the ones needed in the past, not those needed for the dynamic, changing roles of the future.

But identifying talent with the skills needed for the future demands of a job is just the ante to get into the game. Talent development strategies in a complex, diverse, and uncertain world also need to drive toward creativity, commitment, and passion—in other words, heart in addition to head. As noted earlier, the best and the brightest leaders of the future will need to derive meaning from their work and be energized and excited about what they're doing. They will want to feel that their true talents are being used by the company and that they're free to push the envelope with their ideas. And they will want to work in "whole companies" as well as for "whole leaders" who lead with a combination of head, heart, and guts.

Such a whole leadership approach is rarely part of the talent strategy of the large organizations we have seen. Consider the following situations:

• At a leading media company, a senior leader noted that his direct reports were challenging his decisions in a way that had never happened before. He said they weren't content to be told what his decisions were—they wanted to be consulted prior to the decisions. He explained that they weren't hostile about this issue, but they simply wanted to know if other alternatives had been explored. He said that the conversation his people expected is one that he used to have with his peers, not his direct reports, and he felt like he was losing control of his organization.

• Partners in a global financial services firm recently received e-mail from their CEO chastising them for failing to cross-sell the company's services and suggesting they hadn't done so because they lacked a good cross-selling process. The e-mail included an attachment with such a process, a 10,000-word missive that essentially dictated how to cross-sell. The partners found these instructions confusing. As much as this firm talked to its people about empowerment and participatory decision making, this e-mail and others it sent out all seemed to be about obedience. It's a little bit like flying on one of today's airlines and being "welcomed" by the crew!

• Country managers in a large global telephone company are primarily focused on growing their own business unit, rather than the whole company. Their corporation, however, wants to encourage these general managers to develop an "enterprise perspective" and act in the best interests of the whole company, not just their own business. The company knows its future depends on country managers partnering with their scientists, engineers, marketers, and designers to create the next generation of cell phones for emerging markets.

• ABC Corporation is known globally as a place where values count. A great deal of time and effort is invested in communicating these values, and as a result, the company attracts many bright people whose personal values mirror those of the organization. The organization, however, finds that many of its younger people complain that their ideas aren't heard, that they are worked like dogs, that doing what is expedient often supersedes doing what one believes is right. Within a few years, these values-driven recruits become disillusioned and either leave the company or, perhaps even worse, become cynical about it.

The lesson from these examples is that many companies still don't get it. More specifically, they focus on compensation, benefits, and career pathing as discrete elements of a talent strategy. They develop leaders robotically and treat human capital like financial capital. A diverse, engaged workforce, however, needs to be treated with individual differences and talents in mind. Though you can't have ten thousand different assessment, development, and rewards processes for ten thousand employees, you can try and pay attention to what different types of individuals find meaningful about work.

- Some people relish working across functions and business units.
- Others enjoy helping others learn and grow.
- Still others find great satisfaction in being creative.
- Still others can spend all day (and sometimes all night) enmeshed in technological pursuits.

It's time to look at leadership and talent differently. Admittedly, it is more challenging to view it from a head, heart, and guts perspective than simply as an analytical process. But it's also what will give you the edge in recruiting and retaining leaders who are ideally suited for your organization not only for today but also for tomorrow.

OBSTACLES TO DEVELOPING WHOLE LEADERS

We find senior leaders are often confused about what kind of leadership is needed to grow the business and engage people. Most management systems in big companies have seen little true innovation in over a hundred years—since Henry Ford first introduced the assembly line and Frederick Taylor broke down management of people into measurable parts. The result is that most talent developers still view the process from a mechanistic perspective. Unfortunately, that leaves us with companies that are more like machines than organisms, and with talent systems and processes that are inherently more machine-like than organic. In trying to control and measure and fix every aspect of the development process, CEOs and their teams quickly grow frustrated. It can't be done. An organism, however, is an evolving entity. You can't control it—but you can evolve along with it. Therefore, if you approach talent development organically, the process isn't so intimidating. You accept that a program you've designed may become outmoded or that the skill set you identify as crucial for leadership is in continuous flux. You also recognize that you're going to experiment with new ways of learning. This means being willing to test various concepts—such as open-ended dialogue with the CEO, or giving people the option of taking a month off to do pro bono work, or assessment of the key leaders on their use of whole leadership—and see which ones are most viable.

The Costs of Fostering Engagement

Engagement is a big challenge for leaders who are under tremendous pressure to deliver strong quarterly results. Today, most companies have little slack for encouraging development focused on the long term. Every dollar they lose allowing people to take time off to do pro bono work is a dollar they feel they can't afford. At the same time, how many companies today can sustain themselves with uncommitted, uncreative, and uninspired people? What is the cost for an organization where the most innovative people won't accept job offers or won't stay for long? What is the cost of having leaders all cut from the same cloth so people who are different don't aspire to leadership? What is the cost of having employees unable or unwilling to speak up in meetings for fear of retribution from the boss?

A heart strategy can overcome this obstacle, fostering engagement in scores of ways. Determine what really excites and energizes key people, assessing what talents they possess, regardless of whether those talents fit the company's leadership skills profile. Senior executives in heart-sensitive companies get it. They know that when they forge a link between a given employee's talents and assignments, that person becomes engaged in the work like no one else. Whatever the cost of forging this link, it is far outweighed by the resulting productivity.

Pressure from the Financial Community to Deliver Results

The more stress you're under to meet financial goals, the less inclined you are to find ways to provide people with meaningful work. We're not asking anyone to ignore this obstacle; we recognize there are times when you need to push hard and fast and even obsessively to achieve ambitious financial targets. But we are asking you to strike a balance—a balance that can tip one way or another based on what you're dealing with during a given period. By maintaining awareness of the importance of meaningful work, and by making sure your talent management system incorporates this factor into the mix, you stand a decent chance of maintaining a balanced approach between meaning and money.

If you fail to do so, you will create a sterile, by-the-numbers culture. Even leaders at the most results-oriented companies want their people to find fulfillment and be passionate about what they do. They aren't modern-day Simon Legrees cracking the whip and caring not a whit that their people have been turned into drones. Yet because they are so focused and flummoxed by financial pressures to perform, they have the same effect.

More than in any other obstacle, this is where having guts is essential. Going against conventional wisdom—against the belief that making money obviates pursuit of all other goals in uncertain times—requires real courage. An unstated but widespread belief exists that if you want to meet your numbers, you must control your people. Organizations that exercise that sort of control, however, may meet their numbers now, but they are unlikely to meet them in the future. In fact, consider this adage from Ichak Adizes of Corporate Lifecycles: "Growing organizations are focused on flexibility and dying organizations are focused on control." Overly controlling organizations drive the commitment out of their workforce and the meaning out of work. You certainly need to keep some control. But if you don't find a reasonable balance between control and flexibility, you will simply find yourself in firm control of a sinking ship in the perfect storm.

DEVELOPING WHOLE LEADERS ACROSS AN ENTERPRISE

A large financial services institution recently asked us to tell them who among their top hundred leaders had the potential to be on a future executive committee, and who were the real "whole leaders" in this group. They chose sixty high-potential leaders and asked us to assess them, develop them as a group, and provide an individual report on each one of these key leaders as a potential whole leader. We designed an approach that included an intensive action learning experience in which twenty leaders were each assigned to a large team to work on a key issue facing the firm. Among the topics were serving future Hispanic customers, managing risk in the face of terrorism, and developing a modern talent strategy for a "flat world." We provided a battery of whole leader assessment tools for this unique population.

The senior leaders wanted to observe these high-potentials in action, so we also created a business simulation and another experiential activity where they could practice problem solving in a group. We convened some of the best experts on strategy, finance, risk, and management to teach them in the classroom, and we provided each of the participants with intensive coaching on all aspects of leadership during the process. Finally, we wrote a long report on each one, assessing them on their whole leadership potential and recommending follow-up development actions.

Though leaders found this intensive development experience valuable, many said their key learning was recognizing which of their capabilities they relied on and learning to use more than just their guts, or heart, or head in leading. They grew significantly as leaders and stepped up to the challenges of enterprise leadership by being more strategic (head), more open (heart), and more willing to take risks (guts).

The greater value, however, was for the executive committee of the company. We met with them and described the company's leadership DNA in great detail, relying on the assessment data, observations, and action learning team reports of these sixty key leaders.

As a result, we were able to answer essential questions that often go unasked—or are answered incorrectly:

- Why did they have a preponderance of a certain leadership style?
- Why did so many of their leaders exhibit the same personality traits, including the same leadership derailer?
- Why did they, as a company, continue to reward "guts" leaders and not other types of leaders?
- How would future leaders need to look different from this group?
- Which, if any, of this group of sixty leaders could ultimately sit on the executive committee and succeed the current CEO?

This discussion produced some clear insights for these executives. They decided the next step was to develop an approach to talent and leadership that lined up with how complex and uncertain they believed the environment would become. This involved changing the succession planning process. Instead of just focusing on results and past experiences, leaders were also examined in terms of judgment, character, heart, and emotional intelligence. The discussion focused on trying to predict future performance, rather than merely reviewing the data about the past.

In another company, the CEO was interested in finding out who among his group of very senior leaders could lead with head, heart, and guts. He felt if he could spend some significant time with them, he could begin to assess how they thought, reacted, and made important decisions. We facilitated a "Conversation with the CEO" for two days, in which a hand-picked group of leaders got together and talked about key business issues and challenges in an informal and unstructured session. In addition, each of these leaders was assessed, coached individually, and encouraged to build a comprehensive development plan to review individually with the CEO. The conversations focused on enterprise issues facing this company that could not be solved with just head, or heart, or guts: how to engage people more deeply in the work and commit to the future; how to avoid "creeping conservatism" in the culture around risk taking and decision making; how to collectively address cross-business-unit problems such as growing in emerging markets.

The fairy-tale ending to this story would be that this company acquired enterprise leadership at the company level and whole leadership at the individual level from this session. We suspect you know by now, however, that this form of talent development is not a quick fix. It takes systematic development processes and a robust talent process, and this particular company is now putting both in place.

Based on all these examples, we can now identify the three key components to developing whole leaders:

- Assess the "person" underneath the leader.
- Develop leaders three-dimensionally.
- Work with the whole system.

Assess the "Person" Underneath the Leader

Use a variety of assessment tools and methods to understand what makes individual leaders tick—and how to develop them based on that assessment. These tools include intensive assessment by peers, direct reports, and bosses focusing on behaviors and actions, as well as standardized leadership assessments, including a whole leadership assessment, and others focusing on learning agility, derailers, motives, values, style, and preferences. Focus on past experiences but also on judgment, character, decision-making skill, heart, life and career passages, and crucible moments that required guts. We often compile a complete "Whole Leader Report" that depicts and predicts how leaders use their head, heart, and guts.

Develop Leaders Three-Dimensionally

To develop head leadership, focus on new ideas, information, and concepts that are discussed in robust classroom conversations, usually with senior executives who candidly discuss the current and future states.

To develop heart leadership, rely on coaching, 360-degree feedback, and emotional experiences: visiting emerging markets, or surfacing and understanding intense conflicts such as boss-subordinate differences or peer-to-peer fights that engage the emotions but short-circuit the brain. Experiential exercises are also helpful in this regard, particularly those that require teamwork and collaboration.

To develop guts, help people acquire greater understanding of life and career passages, and to leverage what they learn. This includes capitalizing on learning from failure, taking action with uncertain data, participating in simulations that require instant decisions, and most important, carrying out stretch assignments.

Work with the Whole System

Many leaders recognize the importance of whole leadership but complain that the company they work in doesn't support it. They're right. That's why you must involve the CEO and top team in the effort. The way we do this is to focus on the enterprise business challenges a company is facing, and then gain agreement on what kind of leaders are needed. By developing whole leaders around specific business challenges such as growth, capital efficiency, business model changes, innovation, or working globally and asking, How will whole leaders succeed? the process fosters executive involvement.

This involvement follows naturally when the link is made between key business needs and leadership behavior required to meet these needs. For instance, for companies that need greater innovation, what aspects of head, heart, and guts drive greater creativity and disciplined execution of new ideas? Or for companies that have talent and people issues—how can whole leaders engage people differently? In other words, whole leadership is best developed in the context of specific marketplace or internal business challenges, rather than as a stand-alone corporate competency model.

Combine insights about the company with strong data about the leadership pipeline and performance to get executives' attention, buy-in, and sponsorship. From a practical standpoint, taking a whole leadership approach to leadership development is a greater challenge than approaching it in a partial way. No doubt that's why many companies decide to stick to what seems merely difficult but doable. We don't deny that obstacles exist, but we've found that these obstacles can be overcome.

WHOLE LEADERSHIP QUESTIONS TO ASK YOURSELF ABOUT TALENT STRATEGY

Use Your Head
- Has your talent development process remained largely unchanged for the last ten years? Is there anything within that process that assesses what constitutes meaningful work for a given leader or attempts to help that leader find meaning on the job?

- Do you rely on money as your primary or exclusive method to attract and keep talent? Have you ever instituted programs designed to attract and keep talent based on less tangible factors, such as making sure people are allowed to do work on projects that excite them and capitalize on their innate skills?
- Assuming you possess a diverse group of employees, have you assessed what constitutes meaningful work for each group; do you understand what galvanizes your younger employees and what their work preferences are? Do you grasp the factors that are critical for fulfilling work for employees in other countries?

Use Your Heart

- Do you have good intentions when it comes to meaning and talent but poor execution? Do you want to help people find their "sweet spot," but the press of deadlines and decisions causes you to neglect this goal; do you end up focusing exclusively on getting the work done rather than paying attention to how it gets done?
- Do you resent it when people challenge your decisions? Do you find it difficult to understand the values and work styles of people coming into your organization? Have you made an effort to come to terms with these differences and recognize that not everyone has to mirror your generation's values and beliefs?

Use Your Guts

- Do you find it overwhelming to try and develop your people in a meaningful manner? Are you intimidated by the cost and the difficulty? Do you find that you lack the process, the time, or the inclination to do so?

13

Aligning Your Team Around
Whole Leadership

MUCH OF THE WORK OF LEADERSHIP TODAY IS DONE IN TEAMS. Leaders are either members of teams, leading teams, or supporting their boss's team. These teams are absolutely necessary for organizational effectiveness in perfect storms, since (contrary to nautical tradition) one pilot at the helm isn't enough—you need a diversity of voices to arrive at the best course.

Working effectively in teams has become critical for managing complexity, diversity, and uncertainty. Harnessing the power of the enterprise, establishing a clear vision and direction, allocating resources, balancing short- and long-term priorities, planning succession, ensuring execution across units—these all require effective and aligned teams who can work well together.

At the same time, teams present significant challenges for many leaders. Because of their purpose and makeup, teams introduce additional complexity and uncertainty into leadership—the complexity created by the interaction of many personalities and the uncertainty that human behavior always creates in any context. For all the focus on team effectiveness today, few leaders have developed the necessary skills to work well in teams. Many leaders loathe meetings, deride team-building efforts, or just prefer working with one or two others. For leaders who prefer efficiency, control, predictability, and clear outcomes, working in a team is frustrating.

In large, complex organizations, the drive, competitiveness, and control that propel careers and achievements are many times the opposite of what people need to be effective team players. Many leaders excel at driving for results and winning against the competition, but when they bring the same skills to working on a team they sometimes disrupt the team or keep it from being effective. In extreme cases they can derail a team and sometimes the whole company.

We work with many executive committees, but we see few high-performing teams at the top. Instead, they are usually full of efforts to control the dialogue, manage information, or position personal interests—and this is typical even when members like each other. When members are highly competitive and in frequent conflict—not an unusual scenario—lack of trust and poor performance are the norm. We have found that executive teams, like executive leaders, tend to emphasize either head, heart, or guts in their decision-making and personal styles.

Many teams enjoy data analysis; sometimes because this is the leader's preferred style, but mostly because it helps the group reduce complexity. These teams can usually be seen staring at PowerPoint slides and digesting financial or other types of information in 8-point type. Members believe they create value by "trying to figure things out." Other teams tend to be more heart-oriented and focus on how their actions and decisions will affect others, what the organization needs, how people are being treated, or how individual members are responding to each other. When channeled positively, emotional openness results in trust, mutual support, and high performance. When it takes a more negative form, it fosters volatility, conflict, and divisiveness that result in competition and poor team performance. Some teams are clearly guts oriented, and they eschew analysis and pride themselves on "quickly netting things out," acting decisively, and not looking back. But they run the risk of misreading information and even convincing each other they are correct, falling into the meshes of groupthink.

Initial studies of how groups can act reflexively were done in the late 1960s by Irwin Janis, who studied the decisions made during the Cuban missile crisis. President Kennedy forced his team to avoid groupthink by withholding his own opinion and asking for more analysis, encouraging trust in each other's point of view, and forcing each individual to defend his position and insisting that others respond to it. He also frequently left the room, putting his brother Bobby in charge so that everyone would communicate their points of view honestly. In this case, effective team functioning averted World War III.

Leaders can work effectively in teams, but it requires effort and is sometimes counterintuitive (that is, it calls for more than head insights). The complexities of getting aligned action across business units to address superordinate goals are on the agenda of every leadership group today, but most find it a difficult struggle. Why? The trouble begins with the very low expectations many executive team members have about their team's potential performance. They often just expect their agendas to be taken up with trivial matters, and that the real issues will not be dealt with. They may not have a leader who is willing or able to invest the time it takes to create a real team, one whose members are committed to one another's success and who therefore can become a successful team. Or they may simply defer to the wishes of a boss, who usually has strong personal views about what the team is discussing.

But we have found that leading the whole enterprise—company, department, business unit, or function—especially at the top, requires whole leaders who can fully participate with their head, heart, and guts. How do you achieve this today when leaders are stretched so thin—managing multiple complex demands, located in different parts of the globe, and constantly traveling—making it difficult to schedule everyone on the team in one face-to-face meeting?

GETTING THE RIGHT PEOPLE ON THE TEAM

For the whole leader, the most important question is, Who should be on the team? Simple as it sounds, getting the right people in the right room talking about the right issues in the right way is the most important responsibility of a leader—and few do it well. At Avon, Andrea Jung knew that not only would she have to change herself as a leader, the turnaround she was leading would require a different set of skills among members of her leadership team. She brought in leaders who had different capabilities to augment the existing team. The new members brought the focus and discipline required to develop and execute the turnaround plan. Jung says, "We needed a lot of people from the outside. We needed a blend of people who had strong functional expertise but who also knew or could learn quickly our business model."

When Ken Lewis took over as CEO of Bank of America, he executed a similar turnover at the top—changing or removing almost 70 percent of his top executive group within the first two years. He realized that the bank needed to move from a deal-making culture to an execution-focused culture, and this would require a new team with new skills and new ways of working together. CEOs know that their teams should reflect their markets and customers, but few have teams that are anything like that diverse. Tradition, lack of aggressively filling the pipeline with leaders who reflect the changing market, or avoiding the tough decisions needed to change out a team all create this disconnect between intent and action. For example, it is still unusual for U.S. or European global companies to have executive teams that reflect the diversity of their overseas customers.

CREATING VALUE TOGETHER

Once a leadership team is in place, the second issue is how its members create value together. A team of whole leaders must have a simple, clear idea of how they create value as a team. Mindy Grossman, CEO of HSN, says she is "maniacally focused on simplicity, whether it's simplification of strategy, communication, or process. We did an employee survey, and what our employees told us was, as an executive team, what we do has to be incredibly clear, simple, and actionable. So we simplify and communicate very clearly with each person in the company."

Andrea Jung makes the same point in stating that the way to deal with complexity is through "ruthless simplicity." "We focus on fewer, bigger, and better ideas. In the past we stretched the company too thin because of all the initiatives we had. You have to understand your company's capacity to execute. My first four years at Avon our eyes were bigger than our stomachs. We were a culture of a thousand flowers blooming. Now we have three or four big oak trees that everyone can see."

The "oak trees" for an executive team are how they add value as a group. We frequently begin with that key question: How do you as a team add value to the organization? The best predictor of team success is clarity around the purpose of the team. For enterprise teams, we urge the team to think of adding values in three dimensions, as shown in Figure 13.1.

Adding Value from Strategy

An effective executive team should define and drive an overall strategy that goes beyond the simple concatenation of business unit strategies. This includes defining a vision for the company, setting goals and objectives, challenging each other's plans, and allocating resources. All these activities ensure that leaders are operating as a team, rather than just a group.

The classic difference between a group and a team is that a group comes together to report to one another on their individual activities,

FIGURE 13.1. *Value-Adding Role of Executive Teams: Three Key Components.*

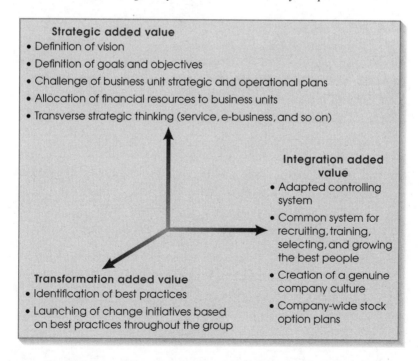

Strategic added value
- Definition of vision
- Definition of goals and objectives
- Challenge of business unit strategic and operational plans
- Allocation of financial resources to business units
- Transverse strategic thinking (service, e-business, and so on)

Integration added value
- Adapted controlling system
- Common system for recruiting, training, selecting, and growing the best people
- Creation of a genuine company culture
- Company-wide stock option plans

Transformation added value
- Identification of best practices
- Launching of change initiatives based on best practices throughout the group

whereas a team comes together to define and achieve a common vision through interdependent work together. Enterprise teams add value when they define their vision and responsibility as something more than the sum of their representative parts.

Adding Value from Transformation

An effective executive team should initiate and drive major changes needed to achieve its strategy, including launching changes, transferring best practices, and focusing on excellence and performance. Change management is one of the most neglected areas of organizational leadership. Most leaders are unaware of the extensive body of knowledge and expertise that can be applied to enabling organizations to change their culture and operating patterns to achieve new organizational goals and initiatives. One fundamental value-added activity of an executive team is to make sure that changes needed in the organization are managed systematically so that the total enterprise tackles challenges in an integrated and effective manner.

Added Value from Integration

An effective executive team should define and steer common policies and key operational processes, such as common recruiting, financial, and training systems. To achieve this, it must also focus on creating a genuine company culture aligned with its strategic needs. This focus on integration is made even more urgent by the diversity of globalization. Establishing a global corporate culture that unites diverse parts of the organization while allowing for local differentiation in execution is one of the most challenging responsibilities in global operations. If the top team does not take up the challenge, however, no other enterprise leadership team can perform this critical activity.

The GRPI Model of Team Performance

Teams must be clear around mission, charter, and objectives. In learning to work together, executive teams must have a clear picture of what comprises high performance and the effective coordination of work between organizational units to achieve clear outcomes. We often use focus on the key aspects of how teams work together to determine where the team can improve. The GRPI model (sketched in Figure 13.2) is useful to help teams identify four key elements of team functioning:

- *Goals:* What is the team trying to accomplish?
- *Roles:* What role does each member play on the team?
- *Processes:* How does the team work together?
- *Interpersonal:* How do team members relate to each other?

It is especially important for executive teams to sort through the complexity of their information, the diversity of their membership, and the uncertainty of their work. We undertake a diagnosis of where a team is working well and where it needs improvement by addressing each element of the GRPI model. We often use a GRPI check

FIGURE 13.2. *GRPI Model of Team Performance.*

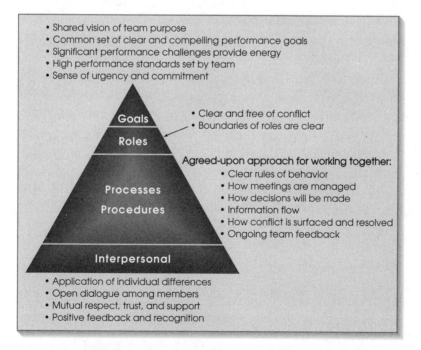

with teams and ask them to rate each of the elements in the figure to define how well they are working together at any given moment. This check allows executive teams, boards, or any other group to quickly and simply assess how clearly they understand the basic building blocks of effective teams—clarity of goals, roles, processes, and relationships.

Developing Trust and Openness

A third issue for executive teams is whether they are willing to commit and support one another's success. Upper-level executives in particular are known for competitiveness and jockeying as they compete for succession to the CEO. Some executive committee members have told us they don't want to appear too vulnerable or too agreeable to others lest they appear "weak" in front of their peers. This fear, of course, is irrational, and we find leaders with real courage or guts are most open to changing their views, listening closely, and allowing themselves to be influenced by others.

High-performing teams are characterized by each member's being fully committed to the success and development of every other member. To do so requires staying open to being influenced. Research by Katzenbach and his colleagues has shown that high-performing teams have to develop trust and openness to help one another for the success of the total enterprise.

We earlier noted the difference between a working group and team. Figure 13.3 sets out the difference between a working group, a team, and a high-performing team.

As an executive, you should have your team periodically rate itself on a scale of 1–10 on the following questions:

- Where are you today as a team?
- Where do you need to be in order to serve customers?
- Where do you need to be to lead the organization?
- Where do you need to be to create value?

The process of rating current state against a desired future provokes open discussion and debate, initiating a process of dialogue that inevitably touches on trust, openness, and commitment to each

FIGURE 13.3.   *Working Group or Team.*

WORKING GROUP	REAL TEAM	HIGH-PERFORMANCE TEAM
A group in which the members interact primarily to share information, best practices, or perspectives and to make decisions to help each member individually perform within a separate area of responsibility.	A small group of people with complementary skills who are equally committed to a common purpose, goals, and working approach for which they hold themselves mutually accountable.	A small group that begins as a real team and outperforms all reasonable expectations given its membership. What makes it high-performing is that its members are deeply committed to one another's personal growth and successes.

Source: Based on Katzenbach and colleagues' research.

other's success. There are times when operating as a working group is perfectly acceptable—and every executive team should agree on when this is an acceptable way to work. But almost all executive committees also need to work as teams if they are to achieve the value-adding goals we noted earlier.

Creating an atmosphere of trust and openness to make good decisions is therefore vital for effective teams. Richard Plepler, co-president of HBO, emphasizes that leaders have to express their viewpoint without fear and to create an environment where others can feel the same way. He says, "It's important to make sure you create an environment where everyone can speak their mind without fear or favor. The test, of course, is whether they say the same things when they leave the room as when you were there."

But this is not always easy. Bill Nelson, CEO of HBO, says that ambiguity creates the conditions for more conflict on a team because by definition answers are not clear or obvious. Multiple viewpoints are frequently all legitimate. The ability to foster debate, listen objectively to all points of view, and be able to arrive at a decision while knowing the uncertainty of the situation are all hallmarks of an effective team.

And Phil Kent, CEO of Turner Broadcasting System, says, "You have to have the right people on your team, including those who will not say 'yes' just to please. And you must have a broad mix of perspectives, for example, someone focused on present revenue streams, someone focused on future revenue streams, someone focused on creative output, and so forth. You have to also recognize that people on the team are motivated by different things. Your job is to make sure that you have the right people in the right jobs and help them all work together towards a common goal."

Leaders work hard to create the conditions for open, honest dialogue. Many leaders struggle with finding the right time to weigh in with their own views—especially if they have already formed a strong opinion and expressing it will naturally curtail further dialogue. Some leaders intentionally hold back, encouraging a more open exchange of ideas. Others leave the room to encourage openness. Bill Weldon, CEO of Johnson & Johnson, invites his executives to give him candid feedback by asking them to discuss the question, "How can I be more effective?" and then leaving the room. They pool their opinions and provide a report on their collective view in an open and frank dialogue when he returns. This takes real guts and is an exercise many leaders are unwilling to undertake. But it fosters the environment of openness teams need to function effectively.

One way to develop a team of whole leaders is to create greater insight into each other's style and preferences. In working with senior teams we use a range of different tools to promote self-awareness and then team awareness. Understanding how different members of a team approach decision making, prefer to resolve conflicts or respond to pressure can give them a "language" to discuss how different styles can be blended into a healthy team climate.

WHOLE LEADERSHIP QUESTIONS TO ASK YOURSELF ABOUT TEAM ALIGNMENT

Peter Senge has said, "Increasingly the talk is the work. Few decisions that lead to action are made unilaterally. Thinking and learning together in fast changing interdependent business settings define successful organizations."

The key skills for whole leaders are using dialogue to convey their head, their heart, or their guts. Here are five ways to facilitate effective dialogue:

1. Surface your overarching purpose—at the heart of your conversations, what do you want people to hear? How much is content and how much is passion and emotion?

What are the two or three fundamental messages you want to communicate for them to identify with (heart) and remember (head)?

2. Open conversation with brief reality checks—what are the key messages or outcomes that need to result? If you know your overarching message, then what are the key outcomes you and others need to look for from your dialogue? What are you trying to achieve together that would be better than each of you could do on your own?

3. Be present—use your head, heart, and guts to fully "show up." When engaging in dialogue be attentive to not only what is being said (head), but how it is said (heart) and the passion and values with which people communicate. Listen for these things in others, and ensure that you are aware of the way you are communicating using your own head, heart, and guts.

4. Engage in a two-way conversation or balance advocacy with inquiry. Leadership today is as much about asking questions as giving answers. In a simpler world leaders could focus on providing answers and demonstrating that they had mastered their responsibilities. But in today's more complex, diverse, and uncertain world, asking the right questions, drawing out others' perspectives, and ensuring that all sides of an issue have been examined will be as important as advocating for your own perspective.

5. Close with forward movement by summarizing, finding, and building on areas of agreement and clarifying understandings and next steps. We have found it amazing how many meetings at the executive level do not check to confirm what will be done as a result of policy discussions. There is very little summarizing of conclusions and defining of next steps. Somehow executives at this level believe those actions should be done by other people concerned with operations. The fact is if people around the table do not check for agreement on their conclusions, each of them in turn will be executing on a different picture of what needs to be done.

These are simple but effective ways to engage in team conversations that lead to decisions and execution. Many team members find it difficult to balance advocacy with inquiry, and what passes for dialogue in many teams is one member advocating one point of view, followed by another member advocating another. But high-powered executive teams use their heads, hearts, and guts to ensure that they are working together for the success of the total enterprise.

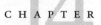

CHAPTER 14

Developing Yourself as a Whole Leader

WE HAVE DISCUSSED SOME OF THE ISSUES ORGANIZATIONS and leaders face when dealing with complexity, diversity, and uncertainty, breaking down those broad issues into nine challenges whole leaders must meet in today's turbulent business world. But navigating the perfect storm is not just about your people or your organization. You are at the helm, and successful navigation will ultimately depend on how well you understand the weather, work with your crew, and manage your emotions and energy to bring your ship into port. This chapter addresses the areas you can work on to ensure that you are capable of becoming a whole leader. CEOs and other leaders we have coached are usually eager to know what they can do on their own to manage complexity, diversity, and uncertainty more effectively, and here we share some of that coaching advice with you.

UNDERSTANDING YOUR LEADERSHIP AGENDA

Start by asking yourself the following question:

What is my leadership agenda?

In other words, what are you trying to accomplish in your current position? What is your overall vision for your company or department?

What are your objectives and your key success factors, and what destination are you attempting to reach? The answers you come up with constitute your leadership agenda. By reflecting on these questions, you can compose a clear statement of what you want to accomplish and for whom you want to accomplish it, along with how you want to get it done. This insight will be important when those around you are confused about the future and are looking to you for guidance in an uncertain world.

A leadership agenda has many aspects. For most executives today, growth is at the top of their leadership agenda—either growth in the market or in their share of the market. In the new financial world we live in after September 2008, credit constraints and huge national debt will cause capital efficiency and cash flow to move much higher on leaders' agendas. Bill McComb, CEO of Claiborne, predicts that leaders in almost every company in every industry will now be even more constrained in the ways they can help it grow, and so will need to focus on efficiencies, return on assets, and inventory turns as important metrics.

For most people, innovation, execution, and serving consumers or customers who have many more choices will also be on the leadership agenda. To form your own leadership agenda, you also have to understand your company's agenda or business priorities, including where it is going to grow, how it is going to organize and do business, and what values it is going to uphold. Linking your leadership agenda to your company's is important for your direct reports and others to see how their activities serve the larger enterprise.

We often ask senior executives to practice communicating their leadership agenda or point of view to others and to receive feedback and coaching based on what they discover. To articulate a leadership agenda, people need to consider how they're going to use their head, heart, and guts when they work with others. As a leader, you need to translate overarching business objectives into goals that are motivating to your people. As we've said, many people do not get up in the morning to achieve a higher return on investment. They come to work to learn, contribute, receive support, be recognized for their contributions, have fun, work hard, and accomplish things they could not accomplish by themselves. They need to be reminded of this—and you as a leader need to make sure that meeting these needs is part of your leadership agenda. If it is not on your agenda, you will not create the kind of climate that motivates workers to give their all to the next crisis or the next revenue objective.

Your leadership agenda needs to be constructed from heart and guts, as well as head.

UNDERSTANDING YOUR LIFE AGENDA

We work with many pharmaceutical executives and often ask them the "why" question around their life purpose and who they serve. Because of sensational media, constant litigation, and political opportunism, many of these executives have assumed a defensive posture. They often initially respond that they want to develop and deliver superior products and services to the health care marketplace, or they want to grow their business so employees and shareholders can be rewarded. Distracted by their daily responsibilities, they sometimes lose sight of the real reason they were first attracted to health care—a life agenda dedicated to serving patients, improving lives, and reducing or eliminating disease. When they are in touch with their life agenda, they are often energized, clear-eyed, and focused on getting things done. When they are reacting to what comes through the inbox or what they read on the Internet, they often become discouraged or depressed.

Your purpose as a leader is tied to the legacy you hope to leave. That legacy may be broad—"I want to save people's lives"—or more narrow, "I intend to develop the talents and skills of those I have the privilege to lead." In either case it is the reason you are willing to put in long hours, read endless e-mails, sit in constant meetings, and suffer through political infighting. It is easy to lose sight of your life agenda, but connecting with it and reminding yourself of it creates energy and stamina.

For all leaders, connecting with their life agenda and linking that to their leadership agenda is the path through the complexity and uncertainty of the perfect storm. As we noted earlier, this is what Stephen Covey calls aligning your "clock" with your "compass." Your clock keeps track of your day-to-day activities, the meetings and priorities through which you run your leadership agenda. But your compass points the direction for your life agenda and ensures that you win the war as well as the battles. Aligning your day-to-day leadership clock with your life compass will not only ensure that you can look back on a fulfilling life but in most instances will also help you keep a steady hand on the helm when life's storms are raging around you—and your people.

Understanding Your Leadership Effectiveness

Most of us have evolved a preferred way of leading, managing, coaching, and working with other people. Our leadership style and behavior is mostly unconscious. Until we attend a leadership program, receive some feedback in a performance review or as part of a development process, or run into a difficult situation that causes us to think about what we are doing, we don't usually have the time or inclination to ask "what kind of leader am I?" We're just too busy leading. The velocity and violence of the perfect storm are also distracting. One challenge of leadership is just maintaining constant consciousness about your behavior.

Start out by reflecting on how you are leading. We often suggest that leaders spend some time every day reviewing their leadership life—meetings they have led, phone conferences they have joined, decisions they have made—and assessing whether they were on their game and how they could have done better.

We once worked with a CEO who wanted to create a "learning organization." He invested a lot of money inviting learning organization specialists to teach his executives how to learn more effectively. In the midst of all this, he hired a new COO, who brought with him a unique management routine. At the end of every meeting or one-on-one session, he would stop the meeting ten minutes from its conclusion to ask a question: "How well did we do during the last fifty minutes [or other time interval]?" The habit of routinely asking that simple question initiated among his direct reports some serious discussion and reflection about how they could improve. Soon, they were asking the same question, and after a while, everyone in the company adopted the habit. The CEO realized he had created a true learning organization with little or no effort or help from outside gurus. Reflection was the key component of learning and improvement.

Ed Koch, when he was mayor of New York City, used to walk around the city and ask everyone the same question: "How am I doing?" Constituents would routinely give him an earful, both good and bad—both helping him improve his performance and making his job easier by helping voters realize that he cared about his performance. Many leaders fail to ask the same question, in some cases because they just don't care about the answer. If you want to become a whole leader and use your head, heart, and guts in a more balanced way, understand with clear-eyed realism how you are leading today.

You can ask about your leadership effectiveness in many different ways and settings—on your own, with an external coach, or as part of a formal leadership development process. If you do it on your own, level the playing field so people can respond candidly. No matter how open and nonjudgmental you might think you are as a supervisor, you always hold some degree of influence over people's careers, performance evaluation, and even pay—and therefore there is always some risk for your team in being candid with you.

A more formal way to assess your leadership is through 360-degree feedback. Feedback instruments are usually based on a company's model of effective leadership and can provide useful insights into how others see you as a leader. We also use a Whole Leadership Head, Heart, and Guts feedback instrument to help leaders understand their primary way of leading other people. Some leaders we have known have also done their own "mini-360" by seeking out feedback from peers, direct reports, and others in a systematic way. Good leaders do this routinely as part of ongoing conversation. Sincerely asking for feedback from others can engage their support of your leadership. However you obtain the information, establish a baseline view of what's working and what's not working in the way you are leading others.

UNDERSTANDING YOUR IMPACT ON OTHERS

We have not yet met a leader who did not have good intentions. In their own mind (or heart of hearts . . . or in their guts), every leader we know is trying to do the right thing, help others, and be effective. If everyone were as effective as they intended, organizations would have no need for leadership development, coaches, programs, or feed-back. If we could compile the intentions of all the executives we have worked with, most companies would experience unlimited growth, delighted customers, and fully engaged employees.

The reality, however, is that a gap often yawns between what leaders intend and the impact they achieve, and unhappy direct reports, dissatisfied customers, and confused bosses soon fall into it. Becoming a whole leader means not seeing the world through your intentions—you must be realistic about how others are responding.

We worked with the CEO of a large global corporation who was asked by his board to obtain some feedback about his impact on others. A board review of his performance had highlighted the fact that he sometimes intimidated others with his critical questioning, focus on details, and rigorous analysis of presentations that were made to him. In interviewing him, we found he was genuinely confused about some of the feedback he had received, because he saw himself as working hard to add value to every interaction. As a typical head leader, he wanted to root out the flaws in arguments of others, so together they could make the best decision. He asked tough questions to find out what was underneath other people's arguments so he could better understand their logic and reasoning. He was comfortable with data and details, and he saw himself using that strength with others to make sure they weren't overlooking an important fact, and that if a decision was made, it would be executed flawlessly.

What he failed to keep in mind was that he was the CEO. The experience of being asked ten tough questions by the CEO, in that ornate office on top of the high-rise, is much different from being asked the same questions by the person in the next cubicle. This CEO could not grasp the impact he had on others simply because of the role he occupied. Only when he began to fully understand the experience others had in his presence could he begin to engage with them at a heart level.

His first step was to acknowledge their experience, and to create some context around his behavior. "I'm not asking these questions to put you on the spot. I just want to understand more of the logic behind your recommendations." That simple statement served to relax others in his presence and open them up to much better dialogue and discussion. The result for this CEO was better opinions and insight from his key people, and ultimately, a board much more satisfied with his performance.

You need to understand not only how people are reacting to you, but why. Fully understanding their experience and reaction to your leadership can help you begin to adopt other strategies for leading. When coaching senior executives, we remind them that their jokes are funnier, their insights are brighter, and their ideas are naturally more insightful than they were the day before they were promoted. Consider what reactions you are obtaining and why. Many senior leaders, especially CEOs, find it difficult to grasp the question because of the constant approval and agreement that surround them each day.

UNDERSTANDING HOW YOU LEARN

To navigate the perfect storm leaders must commit to daily learning. In coaching CEOs we often ask, What do you read each day? What channels do you routinely watch on television? What three books have you completed in the last year? We know that input for leaders shapes their output, and today many leaders forgo a disciplined effort to stay abreast of chosen trends in favor of reacting to the constant stream of information flowing through their world. Many leaders rely on Web sites for information, don't have time to read newspapers, and except on vacation, don't read books or journals. It's difficult to stay informed about a complex, diverse, and uncertain world without taking some time each day to understand and reflect on what is happening around you.

As coaches, we often intervene to suggest leaders create a more disciplined process of learning. Recent approaches to adult learning suggest that people prefer one of four learning styles—experience, reflection, theory, or experimentation. Head-oriented people tend to learn through reading books and articles that present new theories or studying data and information that summarize lessons learned through reflection. Heart-oriented leaders learn through their experience—connecting with people who are different, talking with younger or older people, making an effort to go online with different groups, or going into the cafeteria and lunchroom and getting interested in how others see the world. Visits to India, China, Vietnam, or Brazil create a new context for leaders, especially when they visit consumers' homes, shop in their canteens or stores, attend their sporting or civic events, and connect emotionally with them as people. And guts-oriented leaders enjoy learning most by experimentation—taking risks, trying out new ways of doing things, playing the odds. These leaders usually excel at innovation, but can experiment in the wrong way or at the wrong time and find themselves swept overboard.

It is important to know which learning style is your preference. This does not mean it is the only way you learn, but it may be the most comfortable. This is important for two reasons. First, you will find that you may be vulnerable to important insights that can be gained through learning in a style with which you are not comfortable. For example, a strong analytical leader may miss what customers really want, relying and reflecting on the latest market studies, rather than getting out in the field and experiencing customers' feelings and reactions firsthand. Likewise, a guts-oriented experimenter may wind up in the wrong experiment, having ignored the need to do some homework in advance, which would have warned that the planned action had regularly failed under conditions like the current ones.

Your learning style can be a strength and simultaneously a vulnerability, which brings us to the second reason it is important for you to understand your style—you need to be sure you surround yourself with people whose learning styles complement your own to ensure that you and your team have covered all the bases. It should be obvious that these different styles will bring different insights. In a complex, diverse, and uncertain world all perspectives will be necessary. To be successful, learning organizations need leaders and teams who understand how to learn in different ways.

For many senior leaders, becoming a whole leader requires moving beyond their comfortable existence and typical ways of learning to take in the world in different ways. A coach, a program, an action learning experience can all help. In the end, a leader must commit to working hard each day to stay on the learning edge.

UNDERSTANDING AND MANAGING YOUR ENERGY

Jim Loehr, coauthor of *The Power of Full Engagement,* contends that all personal effectiveness rests on how you first manage your physical energy. Others have talked about working from a "rested edge" rather than a "ragged edge." Those who have studied mind-body relationships almost invariably conclude that it is difficult to perform at world-class standards when you are exhausted.

Managing your physical energy is a bedrock for superior performance. Whether this means managing your health, your fitness, your emotions, or your schedule, you must take seriously that your energy level will ultimately be a significant determinant of your leadership success.

Loehr goes further. He has worked as a sports coach with many of the world's great athletes. Years of experience at this level have convinced him that physical fitness and dexterity are only the foundation of superior performance. On top of good physical conditioning, outstanding performers also understand and manage their emotional, intellectual, and spiritual energy.

We know from experience that personal leadership derailers are all about how you manage your emotional and intellectual energy. Volatile managers derail from emotional immaturity; arrogant managers derail from intellectual immaturity. It is as simple and complicated as that. We also know that derailers are triggered by stress. The perfect storm could not be more stressful. It is incumbent on all leaders therefore to understand and manage their emotional and intellectual energy.

Finally, your spiritual energy goes back to our discussion about your life agenda. Can you and do you identify with some higher purpose or goal toward which your life is directed? And do you keep this in front of you through some form of meditation or spiritual practice? All of these levels of energy need to be managed to be a successful leader in today's complex, diverse, and uncertain world.

WHOLE LEADERSHIP QUESTIONS TO ASK YOURSELF ABOUT YOUR DEVELOPMENT

Use Your Head

- Have you consciously developed a leadership agenda that defines what you need to accomplish in your current position and also what you want to be known for having contributed to your department or organization? What will be your legacy? What will they say about your tenure in this position?
- Are you aware of how others judge your leadership effectiveness and the impact you have on them? Have you received direct feedback from your manager, peers, or direct

reports about your leadership style and how it affects them? Are you aware of the degree to which you rely on your head, heart, or guts in your leadership style? Do you consciously work to use all three in your daily leadership?

Use Your Heart

- When you look back over your life, is there a theme to your life's work? Is there a central idea or a goal you are trying to achieve through different jobs and careers? When you are finished working, will you have a unifying way to describe your cumulative impact on the people and organizations with whom you have worked?

Use Your Guts

- Have you thought about when, where, and how you learn? Do you have a time for reflection that allows you to find shelter from the storm to gather your lessons for the next time out to sea? Do you learn best alone or with others? If with others, have you reached out to the right people to help you learn what is most important to you in your life?
- How well are you managing your energy? Do you try to remain physically fit? Are you managing your relationships to allow you to work at peak emotional energy? Are you keeping up to date with the knowledge you need to excel at your job? Do you find time to gather your thoughts in a way that inspires you to get through the next crisis or challenge in life?

CHAPTER 15

Navigating the Perfect Storm

A Final Thought: Why Whole Leaders Will Succeed

THESE LEADERSHIP CHALLENGES AREN'T GOING AWAY. AS turbulent as the environment is today, they will probably continue. As we write this, the world is experiencing credit contractions, decline in housing values, rising unemployment, economic uncertainties, fluctuating commodity prices, terrorist bombings, and continued fear and uncertainty about the future. If that sounds like doom and gloom, it isn't our intent. Instead, we fully believe the challenges of complexity, diversity, and uncertainty can be met, no matter how chaotic and confusing things become. We have great faith in the abilities of whole leaders to meet whatever challenges they face.

What we don't have as much faith in is the idea that people will embrace whole leadership. Most of us lean toward head, heart, or guts leadership. If we're facing an especially difficult problem or big opportunity, our inclination is to lead with our strength. Head leaders become even more analytical than they normally are; heart leaders become more active in seeking solutions through other people; guts leaders place greater reliance on their point of view and use it to take significant risks.

No matter how many surprises occur or how difficult a situation gets, whole leaders possess an almost unlimited capacity to deal with whatever comes their way. They really are three-in-one leaders, and that tops a partial leader, no matter how proficient in the preferred leadership mode. We'll take someone who has good head, heart, and guts skills over the smartest guy in the room every day of the week. Here's why.

Imagine how complex, diverse, and uncertain your business has become in recent years. Now double it. Or triple it. Only a three-tool leader can function effectively in this type of future environment. Perhaps you question whether things really will become this complex, diverse, and uncertain in the future. If so, consider taking a look at the future that we believe is just around the corner.

Too Much Speed, Too Many Surprises, Too Little Time to Decide

Some business models are under siege today, and every model will be under siege in the next five to ten years. Consider what has happened to the pharmaceutical model and overlay those changes on any industry you choose. Think about the financial services industry and how it has failed to deal effectively with the complexity of financial instruments and credit—and about the price that has been extracted since September 2008. What will happen if the price of oil continues its wild fluctuations, or if the focus on alternative fuels such as ethanol drives the price of corn even higher than it is as of this writing? On top of all this, more players from around the world will be entering markets and competing successfully because of their lower costs for labor and transportation of natural resources. New technological breakthroughs will alter everything from relationships to product materials to the speed at which things are done.

Now take a breath. While we could go on for pages about all the factors that will make the future more complex, diverse and uncertain, here we narrow our focus to the key issues that are on the horizon:

- *Technology versus ethics.*

Biotechnology, nanotechnology, neurotechnology, and information technology are creating great product advances, especially in the medical sciences, but we are also starting to see how these new technologies will soon raise ethical dilemmas. Speculation has already begun that nanotechnology may produce asbestos-like products that can carry carcinogens to every organ in the body. With the continued use of information technology, private information is more likely to be collected and collated for someone unauthorized to view, or of more concern, to be hacked and shared without permission. Already we've seen cases where credit card information and medical and employment histories have been stolen by hackers. Invariably, lawsuits will be filed against the companies this private information is stolen from. What is the right thing to do? The profitable thing?

How much due diligence does a company owe society before launching a breakthrough product that may cause serious health problems and simultaneously save millions of lives? What is the responsibility owed to the large majority who can be helped by a medical device? Is it equal to the responsibility for safety owed to the tiny fraction likely to be harmed? Do companies creating advances in cell therapy need to be concerned about harvesting stem cells? How many firewalls at what cost should companies build to protect private data—what's reasonable and what's financially feasible?

• *Micromarketing versus the soul of the brand.*

Nike already has thousands of micro markets to talk to, manage, and develop products for. Levi's customizes jeans online to fit a variety of body types and sizes. User groups, patient advocacy groups, consumer organizations, and even fan clubs all communicate with companies and celebrities in a continuous feedback loop. We're moving toward an era where people feel like they're starring in their own movies and expect products and services tailored to their own idiosyncratic needs and tastes. Using various technologies—blogs, e-mail, Web sites, podcasts—organizations are starting to learn how to communicate with these micromarkets. The problem, of course, is that branding is also becoming increasingly important. How do you tailor communication to thousands of markets and maintain the soul of the brand? How can you run a network television commercial that doesn't contradict all those micro messages?

• *The changing nature of diversity.*

Throughout this book, we've talked about diversity in present terms, but in the future, diversity may no longer be viewed in group terms but on an individual basis. In keeping with the micromarketing trend just discussed, it's difficult today to talk about Chinese or Hispanics or women or seniors as one homogeneous entity. Everything is fragmenting; it's already reached the point where a group such as Swedish men aged thirty-five to forty-five who drive Volvos is no longer viable as a target market. Instead, you need to target Sven from Malmo who likes red Volvos with green seats. Internally, dividing your workforce into blacks, whites, Hispanics and other traditional categories will no longer make sense. Each group has so much internal variation in terms of requirements and preferences that meeting the diverse needs of a workforce becomes a monumental challenge. Diversity today tends to be a matter of empathy, of connecting with different groups who may not be like you. This is a heart capability. In the future, though, as diversity becomes an individual proposition, it will also become a matter for the head—gaining an intellectual understanding of the thousands of micro groups with whom you interact.

- *The paradox of analysis.*

As the world's complexity increases, organizations are going to become more reliant on analysis to figure things out. Unlike the past, however, in the future the astonishing complexity of things will defy analysis, at least to a certain extent. We know of one media company that almost destroyed its publications by relying too heavily on focus groups to assess its market. Emerging trends advanced on its publications relentlessly and from every direction. Focus groups kept bringing up new points that the company then researched, analyzed, and strategized. Pretty soon, it was caught in a spider's web of information strands. Rather than relying on their instincts—on their theory of the case or belief about the way things should work—the company's leaders became overwhelmed and overinfluenced by information.

Striking a balance between an analytical approach and an instinctive one will be even more critical in the future. There's going to be more complexity to unravel through analysis, and much of that complexity will be too overwhelming to deal with in a logical, fact-based manner.

- *A never-ending series of surprises.*

There's no need to tell you that the world has become a smaller place and that what happens halfway across the world can have a profound effect on a small company in Iowa. What we do need to tell you is that this interconnectedness creates surprises. You may walk into work one day and find that people already know about a planned corporate downsizing even before you do—the CEO mentioned it to his spouse who told a cousin who told a friend who put it on the Web. Your emerging market supplier may come under international scrutiny for a series of payoffs to business executives and government officials and your company is tainted by association. A ten-person company may come up with a technological innovation that renders your billion-dollar business obsolete. Some of these surprises, of course, can be positive. That tiny ten-person company might form an alliance with you and together allow you to dominate the market. Our point is that uncertainty is bound to increase in an increasingly interconnected world.

HOW WHOLE LEADERS CAN RESPOND: THREE WAYS TO MEET THE CHALLENGES OF THE PERFECT STORM

Think about some of the challenges we've discussed: Blowing up your business model, turning green without bleeding red, leading an unfamiliar workforce, relying on what you believe in. These challenges are impossible to meet if you only rely on your head, your heart, or your guts. Because of the increasing turbulence of your environment, your brilliant analysis will be rendered useless. If you don't have another way of dealing with a challenge in the future—if you can't deal with it through your relationships or through your beliefs—then you're out of luck.

Whole leadership allows you to act in three ways that are important now but absolutely essential in the future. Let's examine what they are and why they are so useful in volatile, unpredictable environments:

- Act authentically.
- Balance money and meaning.
- Develop the capacity to connect.

Act Authentically

During the Democratic primary race between Barack Obama and Hillary Clinton, we saw an eye-opening example of what can happen when a whole leader responds authentically to a particularly difficult situation. As you may recall, the defining moment of Senator Obama's campaign occurred when his then-pastor, Reverend Jeremiah Wright, gave a sermon that struck some people as racially divisive and even anti-American. Senator Obama was placed in an enormously difficult position: denounce Wright and alienate a significant part of his constituency or say nothing and risk alienating another significant part of his constituency.

If Senator Obama had merely analyzed the situation with his head, one option would probably have edged forward as the least damaging and he would have chosen accordingly. Instead, he gave a speech where he spoke from the heart and the head—and with a tremendous amount of guts. His message was that he rejected the divisive comments, but that he was not about to turn his back on someone whom he considered a friend and good person. During his speech, Obama brilliantly analyzed the situation, demonstrated empathy for his minister, and had the courage to speak from a position of belief—a belief that you can condemn a friend's action but that you don't condemn a friend for a single action.

During the weeks that this controversy occurred, Obama's speech was the most downloaded video on YouTube. This is astonishing in and of itself—how many other recent politicians can you think of who had their speeches downloaded—but it also offers testimony to the power of acting authentically. More than anything else, that's what came through in this speech. It was clear that he was speaking from the head, from the heart, and with guts, and when that happens, a sense of authenticity is conveyed.

Authenticity will be a prized leadership quality in the coming years. As people in organizations forge multiple relationships with each other and with external sources of information through technology, they will spot fakes faster. In the past and even today, some leaders attempt to get away with what we refer to as "smiling generalities." They tell their people "we're all family" or that the company has no plans to sell off a division. Yet through chat rooms and online forums, people can quickly assess if these blandly optimistic statements are accurate.

Perhaps just as significantly, a growing need exists on the part of all employees for the truth. For a long time, leaders have lied about or sugar-coated unpleasant truths. They have acted the part they thought they must play to be good leaders. Today and even more in the future, the bar is being raised on authenticity. The more confusing and uncertain the world becomes, the more people want leaders who are real. In organizations, people may not be sure if they'll have jobs tomorrow or even if their company will look the same. What helps, however, is knowing that their CEO will be exactly the person they expect, will respect them enough to be authentic, and will deserve their continuing respect.

Authenticity earns leaders respect. Barack Obama appears to be a genuine leader. That quality, much more than his policies and programs, is what attracted so many people to his candidacy. During his Reverend Wright speech, he noted that his white grandmother had made racial slurs against blacks on occasion, but that he didn't disown her because of them; he understood who she was and that in many ways, she was a wonderful person.

Few politicians have the courage to be so open, vulnerable, and compassionate at the same time—all of which comes together as authenticity.

Balance Money and Meaning

Many of the challenges we've discussed involve paradox—for example, how to turn green without bleeding red. At the root of many of these paradoxes is the pull between doing what's right in the long run and the push of doing what makes money now.

Leaders are confronting what we refer to as the *money-meaning gap,* and the future will only make this gap wider and more difficult. Emphasis on profits increasingly conflicts with all the factors that make work a relevant, purposeful, values-based endeavor. To survive and thrive in the next ten to twenty years, organizations will have to make "gap management" a priority. This is difficult to do, of course, because of the crushing pressure for short-term results. Obviously, you can't ignore financial requirements. At the same time, however, you can't let them blind you to the growing importance of meaning.

What is meaning? On one level, it is about the significance of work. Does everyone from senior leaders to new employees feel fulfilled and proud of what they are trying to accomplish? Do they believe they are working for an organization whose values mirror their own? While people still want well-paid, prestigious jobs with top companies, the traditional rewards of work are no longer enough for a growing number of employees. They want to believe that what they do matters—that it has purpose.

On a second level, as noted in Chapter Eight, meaning is about social responsibility, fueled by the green movement, the increasing emphasis on diversity, and the growing governmental insistence worldwide that organizations be good corporate citizens. Companies like the Body Shop and Ben & Jerry's have made large and sincere commitments to causes, and these commitments are meaningful to many stakeholders—the media, customers, employees, and government agencies. On the other hand, it is not particularly meaningful when a CEO makes a token contribution to a philanthropic group or sponsors a not-for-profit group's march. Stakeholders have become much more sophisticated about distinguishing truly meaningful efforts from sops thrown in the direction of a good cause.

We must also recognize that what is meaningful can also vary from company to company, based on a given industry, culture, and tradition. Consider the pharmaceutical business. Commitment to patients is a natural component of meaning in this industry. Yet this commitment has been eroded because of the intense focus on profits. Too often, companies are developing the products that will yield the highest profits rather than the ones that society really needs. Some pharma companies have had to be pressured by government and other activist groups to research, develop, or distribute low-profit (or no-profit) drugs that deal with social ills, such as the AIDS crisis in Africa. A good PR campaign may attempt to persuade the world that a company has a social conscience, but skeptics may believe this company's conscience is as ephemeral as the e-mailed news release that announced its self-proclaimed noble deed. What is the truth? Is a company sincere in its efforts to provide drugs to the world's needy or is it simply good publicity? For some who believe in the company's good intentions, the money-meaning gap may be narrow. For skeptics, though, the gap may be wide.

Clearly, this is an enormously complex issue that leaders need to consider within the context of their own organizations. But it's an issue that's not going to go away. To win the war for talent, to build brands, to function effectively in a global environment—all this involves managing meaning.

Develop the Capacity to Connect

The best leaders in the future will be connectors and collaborators, not just in terms of bringing people together but also allying disparate ideas and organizations. *Interdependence* is the watchword for the future, and people who can facilitate connections will have a huge advantage over those who can't.

This means being able to connect the dots—to figure out how seemingly unrelated concepts or views can be brought together in a synergistic whole. This is what Steve Jobs did with the iPhone, but there are many non-product-related examples of connect-the-dots thinking. Car companies provide financing; banks offer insurance, advice, mortgages, and investments; real estate rental agencies now provide concierge services including baby-sitting, catering, and dog walking. In each case, the dots are extended to include bundling of additional features and services.

Connecting also can mean bringing a diverse group of people together to work toward the same end. This can be a huge challenge for global organizations (recall our challenge of leading people who aren't like you) and it requires heart capacities. But it also demands astute analysis to select the right groups for an alliance, as well as guts to gather untraditional or unorthodox groups under the same roof based on your belief that they are the ones who can make your goal a reality.

Many leaders today can connect only in one way. They are good at connecting intellectually with others on the basis of facts or strategy. They are adept at forming and maintaining strong relationships. Or they are proficient at using their values and beliefs to forge connections. In the future, though, leaders must possess all three of these connecting capabilities. They must be able to think, feel, and take chances based on the myriad potential connecting points that exist in any business universe. The best leaders will know how, when, and why to connect their particular set of dots.

CONTINUOUS ASSESSMENT FOR CONTINUOUS LEARNING

Acting authentically, balancing meaning and money, and connecting are going to be of paramount importance, but we also highly recommend one other ability for anyone gazing into an uncertain future.

The challenges we've presented are not static. As they evolve, your leadership capacity must follow suit. As we've emphasized, whole leaders are nothing if not adaptable. By using head, heart, and guts, they keep themselves from becoming locked into a singular approach.

Yet how do whole leaders stay adaptable? How do they avoid the all-too-human trap of resting on their laurels, relying on an approach that has brought them success?

As the heading of this section suggests, continuous assessment for continuous learning is the answer. Many leaders profess to be learners, but they're not. They talk about how they're open to new experiences and how they truly intend to use the 360-degree feedback they receive, but they fail to do so. In their own minds, they may be convinced that they are learners, but if you watch them, you don't see any behavioral change, any willingness to say "I don't know" or to test a new approach. In organizations that expect leaders to be confident and definitive in their decisions, it is difficult for people to question themselves and admit when they aren't sure what to do.

The leaders who can, though, are the ones who are positioning themselves to develop and grow. They are constantly expanding their head, heart, and guts capacities. Self-assessment is the catalyst for this expansion. And it's not just assessing today's abilities today; it requires assessing those abilities against future needs. They frequently assess their values and beliefs—will their truths today be valid a few years down the road? They look at their trustworthiness, their ability to communicate with others in ways that are important to those people (rather than to themselves). They think about their character, not just their subject knowledge or analytical skills. They honestly reflect upon whether who they are fits with what their organization will need.

All this mirrors a paradigm shift taking place in the best organizations. It used to be that companies relied on business formulas to achieve success, but now they are increasingly interested in new assessment and development technologies. They grasp that the true differentiator is talent, and that organizations that find ways to attract, keep, and grow their top people are the ones that will achieve a real competitive edge.

Meeting the challenges we've discussed isn't easy today, and it's going to be even more difficult in the future. Preparing yourself and others to meet them requires a commitment to rigorous, continuous assessment and learning from that assessment. In a world that is becoming increasingly complex, diverse, and uncertain daily, it is a commitment that whole leaders willingly embrace.

Bibliography

"As Oil Giants Lose Influence, Supply Drops." *New York Times* (August 19, 2008): A1.

Ashkenas, Ron. "Simplicity-Minded Management." *Harvard Business Review* 85, no. 12 (2007): 101–109.

Badaracco, Joseph L., Jr. *Defining Moments: When Managers Must Choose Between Right and Right.* Boston: Harvard Business School Press, 1997.

Banaji, M. R., Bazerman, M., and Chugh, D. "How (Un)Ethical Are You?" *Harvard Business Review* 81, no. 12 (2003): 56–64.

Bartlett, Christopher, and Sumantra Ghoshal. "Matrix Management: Not a Structure, a Frame of Mind." *Harvard Business Review* (July–August 1990): 138–145.

Bhattacharya, Ashis. "Chasing the Elephant." *Economist* 382, no. 8512 (January 20, 2007): 65–66.

Birkinshaw, Julian, and Cristina Gibson. "Building Ambidexterity into an Organization." *MIT Sloan Management Review* 45, no. 4 (Summer 2004): 47–55.

Brinkley, Amy Woods. "Unambiguous Leadership in Ambiguous Times." *Vital Speeches of the Day* 73, no. 12 (December 2007): 531–533.

Business in the Community. *Benchmarking Responsible Business Practice.* London: Business in the Community, May 2007.

Cameron, Kim, Robert Quinn, Jeff DeGraff, and Anjan Thakor. *Competing Values Leadership: Creating Value in Organizations.* Northampton, Mass.: Edward Elger, 2006.

Camillus, John C. "Strategy as a Wicked Problem." *Harvard Business Review* 86, no. 5 (2008): 98–106.

Canton, James. *The Extreme Future: The Top Trends That Will Shape the World in the Next 20 Years.* New York: Penguin, 2006.

Ciampa, Dan, and Michael Watkins. *Right from the Start: Taking Charge in a New Leadership Role.* Boston: Harvard Business School Press, 2005.

Clampitt, Phillip G., and Robert DeKoch. *Embracing Uncertainty: The Essence of Leadership.* London: Sharpe, 2001.

Climate Counts. *Climate Scorecard.* Manchester, N.H.: Climate Counts, May 2007.

Collins, James. *Good to Great.* New York: HarperCollins, 2001.

Collins, James, and Jerry Porras. *Built to Last: Successful Habits of Visionary Companies.* New York: HarperCollins, 1994.

Covey, Stephen M. R. *The Speed of Trust.* New York: Free Press, 2006.

Covey, Stephen R., A. Roger Merrill, and Rebecca Merrill. *First Things First: To Live, to Love, to Learn, to Leave a Legacy.* New York: Free Press, 1996.

Covin, Geoffrey. "What Makes GE Great?" *Fortune* 153, no. 4 (March 6, 2006): 90–96.

Coyne, Kevin P., Patricia Gorman Clifford, and Renee Dye. "Breakthrough Thinking from Inside the Box." *Harvard Business Review* 85, no. 12 (2007): 70–78.

Day, George, and Paul Shoemaker. "Are You a 'Vigilant Leader'?" *MIT Sloan Management Review* 49, no. 3 (Spring 2008): 43–51.

Deming, W. Edwards. *Out of Crisis.* Cambridge, Mass.: MIT Press, 1986.

Dotlich, David, and Peter Cairo. *Unnatural Leadership: Going Against Intuition and Experience to Develop Ten New Leadership Instincts.* San Francisco: Jossey-Bass, 2002.

Dotlich, David, James Noel, and Norman Walker. *Leadership Passages: The Personal and Professional Transitions That Make or Break a Leader.* San Francisco: Jossey-Bass, 2004.

Dupras, Laurence. "Green for 'Go.'" *Supply Chain Standard* (February/March 2008).

Earley, P. Christopher, and Elaine Mosakowski. "Cultural Intelligence." *Harvard Business Review* 82, no. 10 (2004): 139–146.

Edmondson, Gail. "BMW Hits a Speed Bump." *Business Week Online* (August 1, 2007).

Eisenstat, Russell, Michael Beer, Nathaniel Foote, Tobias Fredberg, and Flemming Norrgren. "The Uncompromising Leader." *Harvard Business Review* 86, no. 7/8 (2008): 130–131.

Estrin, Judy. *Closing the Innovation Gap: Reigniting the Spark of Innovation in a Global Economy.* New York: McGraw-Hill, 2008.

Esty, Daniel C. "Transparency: What Stakeholders Demand." *Harvard Business Review* 85, no. 10 (2007): 30, 34.

George, Bill. *True North: Discover Your Authentic Leadership.* San Francisco: Jossey-Bass, 2007.

"Global CEO Study: The Enterprise of the Future." *IBM* (May 2008).

Goffee, Rob, and Gareth Jones. "Managing Authenticity: The Paradox of Great Leadership." *Harvard Business Review* 83, no. 12 (2005): 87–94.

Grove, Andrew. *Only the Paranoid Survive.* New York: Time Warner, 1999.

Gwyther, Matthew. "How to Survive Complexity." *Management Today* (London) (April 2008): 36–41.

Heifetz, Ron. *Leadership Without Easy Answers.* Boston: Harvard University Press, 1994.

Hollis, James. *Finding Meaning in the Second Half of Life.* New York: Gotham, 2006.

Holstein, William J. "Why Wal-Mart Can't Find Happiness in Japan." *Fortune* 156, no. 3 (August 6, 2007): 73–78.

Hunter, Debra. "Resilience and Tolerance for Ambiguity in Crisis Situations." *Business Review* (Cambridge) 5, no. 1 (September 2006).

"In Search of a Good Company." *Economist* (September 8, 2007): 65–66.

"Inside Smart Decisions." *Business Week,* no. 4059 (November 19, 2007): 70–71.

Iyer, Bala, and Thomas H. Davenport. "Reverse Engineering Google's Innovation Machine." *Harvard Business Review* 86, no. 9 (September 2008): 131.

Johnson, Barry. *Polarity Management: Identifying and Managing Unsolvable Problems.* Amherst, Mass.: Human Resource Development Press, 1996.

Kalev, A., F. Dobbin, and E. Kelly. "Best Practices or Best Guesses? Assessing the Efficacy of Corporate Affirmative Action and Diversity Policies." *American Sociological Review* 71 (2006): 589–617.

Katzenbach, Jon, and Douglas Smith. *The Wisdom of Teams: Creating a High Performance Organization.* Boston: Harvard Business School Press, 1993.

Koestenbaum, Peter. *Leadership: The Inner Side of Greatness.* San Francisco: Jossey-Bass, 1991.

Kolb, David A. *The Learning Styles Inventory,* Version 3.1. Boston: Hay Resources Direct, 2005.

Lafley, A. G., and Ram Charan. *The Game Changer.* New York: Crown Business Books, 2008.

Lahiri, Somnath, Liliana Perez-Nordtvedt, and Robert W. Renn. "Will the New Competitive Landscape Cause Your Firm's Decline? It Depends on Your Mindset." *Business Horizons* 51, no. 4 (July–August 2008): 311.

Lawrence, Paul, and Nitin Nohria. *Driven: How Human Nature Shapes Our Choices.* San Francisco: Jossey-Bass, 2002.

Lissack, Michael, and Johan Roos. *The Next Common Sense: Mastering Corporate Complexity Through Coherence.* London: Nicholas Brealey, 2000.

Loehr, James, and Tony Schwartz. *The Power of Full Engagement: Managing Energy, Not Time, Is the Key to High Performance and Personal Renewal.* New York: Free Press, 2003.

Maak, Thomas. "Responsible Leadership, Stakeholder Engagement and the Emergence of Social Capital." *Journal of Business Ethics* 74, no. 4 (September 2007): 329–343.

Martin, Roger. "How Successful Leaders Think." *Harvard Business Review* 85, no. 6 (2007): 60–67.

Olsen, Matthew, and Derek van Bever. *Stall Points: Most Companies Stop Growing–Yours Doesn't Have To.* New Haven, Conn.: Yale University Press, 2008.

Peters, Tom, and Robert Waterman. *In Search of Excellence: Lessons from America's Best Run Companies.* New York: HarperCollins, 1982.

"Q&A with Mark Hurd." *Baylor Business Review* (Waco, Tex.) 25, no. 1 (Fall 2006): 26–29.

Reilly, David. "Center of a Storm: How CEOs Work." *Wall Street Journal* (June 23, 2007): B1.

"Retail Banking: Lateral Thinking and Agility Are Essential in a Changing World." *Banker* (London) (May 2008).

Rhinesmith, Stephen H. "Learning to Live with Paradox: A Manager's Guide to the Survival of the Most Cooperative." *Mercer Management Journal,* no. 20 (2005): 65–69.

Roquebert, Jaime, Robert L. Phillips, and Peter A. Westfall. "Markets vs. Management: What 'Drives' Profitability?" *Strategic Management Journal* 17, no. 8 (1996): 653–664.

Sachs, Jeffrey. *Common Wealth: Economics for a Crowded Planet.* New York: Penguin, 2008.

Salanick, Gerald, and James Meindl. "Corporate Attributions as Strategic Illusions of Management Control." *Administrative Science Quarterly* 29 (1984): 238–254.

Samuelson, Judith. "Green Stakeholders: Pesky Activists or Productive Allies?" HBR Green Online Discussion About Leadership and the Environment (March 2008). Available online: www.hbrgreen.org/2008/03/green_stakeholders_pesky_activ.html. Access date: January 6, 2008.

Schumpeter, Joseph. "Creative Destruction." In *Capitalism, Socialism and Democracy.* New York: HarperCollins, 1975. (Originally published 1942.)

See, Thomas, and Laura Sue D'Annunzio. "Challenges and Strategies of Matrix Organizations: Top-Level and Mid-Level Managers' Perspectives." *HR Human Resource Planning* (New York) 28, no. 1 (2005): 39–49.

Shoemaker, Paul. *Profiting from Uncertainty: Strategies for Succeeding No Matter What the Future Brings.* New York: Free Press, 2002.

Shrader, Ralph W. "Leadership in a Liquid World." *MIT Sloan Management Review* 49, no. 1 (Fall 2007): 96.

Sirkin, Harold, James Hemerling, and Arindam Bhattacharya. *Globality: Competing with Everyone from Everywhere for Everything.* Boston: Business Plus, 2008.

Slywotzky, Adrian. *Value Migration.* Boston: Harvard Business School Press, 1996.

Slywotzky, Adrian. *The Upside: From Risk Taking to Risk Shaping—How to Turn Your Greatest Threat into Your Biggest Growth Opportunity.* New York: Wiley, 2007.

Slywotzky, Adrian, David Morrison, and Bob Andelman. *The Profit Zone: How Strategic Business Design Will Lead You to Tomorrow's Profit.* New York: Times Business, 1997.

Snowden, David, and Mary Boone. "A Leader's Framework for Decision Making." *Harvard Business Review* 85, no. 11 (2007): 69–76.

Steger, Ulrich, Wolfgang Amann, and Martha Maznevski. *Managing Complexity in Global Organizations.* New York: Wiley, 2007.

Tapscott, Dan, and Anthony Williams. *Wikinomics: How Mass Collaboration Changes Everything.* USA: Portfolio, Penguin Group, 2006.

Taylor, Rodney. "Turning up the Heat." *Risk Management* (New York) 55, no. 7 (2008): 30–35.

Tedlow, Richard S. "Leaders in Denial." *Harvard Business Review* 86, no. 7/8 (2008): 18–19.

Veleva, Vesela. *Time to Get Real: Closing the Gap Between Rhetoric and Reality* (research report). Boston: Boston College Center for Corporate Citizenship, December 2007.

Weick, Karl E., and Kathleen M. Sutcliffe. *Managing the Unexpected: Resilient Performance in an Age of Uncertainty,* 2nd ed. San Francisco: Jossey-Bass, 2007.

Welch, Jack, and Suzy Welch. "It's Insular at the Top: Did Chuck Prince and Stan O'Neal Lose Touch with the Companies They Ran?" *Business Week* podcast, no. 4059 (November 19, 2007): 120.

Wheatley, Margaret. *Leadership and the New Science: Discovering Order in a Chaotic World,* 3rd ed. San Francisco: Berrett-Koehler, 2006.

Acknowledgments

This book could not have been written without the insights and ideas we have gained from talking with and observing many great leaders around the world. We have had the privilege of working with many outstanding executives as they have led their organizations through complexity, diversity, and uncertainty with skill and resilience. Many of these individuals were also gracious enough to share their ideas with us in conversations about these topics: Bill Weldon, CEO of Johnson & Johnson; Andrea Jung, CEO of Avon Products; Ian Cook, CEO of Colgate-Palmolive; Mark Parker, CEO of Nike; Dick Clark, CEO of Merck; Angela Ahrendts, CEO of Burberry; YM Park, CEO of Doosan Infracore; Allen Lew, CEO of SingTel Singapore; Mindy Grossman, CEO of HSN; Brenda Barnes, CEO of Sara Lee; Phil Kent, CEO of Turner Broadcasting; Bill McComb, CEO of Claiborne; Gregg Steinhoffel, CEO of Target; Rodger Lawson, CEO of Fidelty; Marty Carroll, CEO of Boehringer-Ingelheim; Bill Nelson, CEO of HBO; Richard Plepler, co-president of HBO; John Huey, editor-in-chief of Time, Inc.; Colleen Goggins, J&J worldwide president of consumer products; Charles MacCormack, president of Save the Children; and Ken Frazier, president of global human health for Merck.

In addition, other leaders have taught us much more than we could put into this book: Kaye Foster-Cheek, Russ Deyo, Harlan Weisman, Nick Valeriani, Corey Seitz, Barbara Elbertson, Larry Kaye, Jonathan Rosin, Jennifer Harnden, Dan Ciampa, Jim Shanley, Zhrengong Liu,

Frank Waltmann, Yolanda Hofer, Mirian Graddick-Weir, Ann Tidball, Steve Mostyn, Shlomo Ben-Hur, Fons Trompenaars, Mansour Javidan, John Naisbitt, David Frediani, Jane Blankenship, Charlie Denson, Eric Sprunk, Jill Stanton, David Ayre, Mike Tarbell, Debbie Bishop, Stephen Cerrone, Jodee Kozlak, Daniel Marsili, Lucien Alziari, Evelyn Rodstein, Joan Gutkowski, and Vera Vitels.

Many colleagues have especially helped us deliver on our commitments so we could write this book: Ron Meeks, Stacey Philpot, Bev Burton, Albertina Dubrowsky, Jennifer Gardiner, Charlie Miller, Annette Thum, Christina Mott, and the many coaches and faculty who work with us each week in senior executive programs.

Finally, this book would not have been completed without the consistent and superb help of a few key people: Michaelene Kyrala, Julie Aiken, Julie Roberts, Sako Matsui, Bruce Wexler, and especially the Wiley team: Cedric Crocker, Rebecca Browning, Mary Garrett, and Gayle Mak. Thank you all for persisting through the complexity and uncertainty that writing this book has required.

About the Authors

David L. Dotlich, Ph.D., is an adviser, author, researcher, teacher, and speaker on leadership, business strategy, developing high potential, and succession. He is coauthor of nine best-selling books, including *Why CEOs Fail* and *Action Learning,* and is editor of the *Pfeiffer Leadership Development Annual,* which yearly compiles the thinking and best practices in leadership development. He is the founder and former president of the Oliver Wyman Executive Learning Center and was formerly executive vice president of Honeywell International. He is an adviser to CEOs, executive committees, and boards in companies such as Johnson & Johnson, Nike, Fidelity, Sara Lee, Target, Toshiba, HSN, and Kraft. He has been named one of the Top 50 Coaches in the United States.

Peter C. Cairo, Ph.D., is a senior partner at Oliver Wyman and a consultant who specializes in the areas of leadership development, executive coaching, and executive team effectiveness. He spent twenty years as a full-time faculty member at Columbia University, where he served as chairman of the Department of Organizational and Counseling Psychology. Dr. Cairo has been a primary consultant and coach to numerous senior executives and leadership teams at Time Warner, Colgate-Palmolive, Avon Products, Citigroup, Boehringer-Ingelheim, KPMG, Bank of America, and The Carlyle Group, where he and his colleagues have also developed and delivered executive leadership programs. He is coauthor of several books, including *Why CEOs Fail: The 11 Behaviors That Can Derail Your Climb to the Top and How to Manage Them.*

Stephen H. Rhinesmith, Ph.D., is a senior partner at Oliver Wyman, a firm that specializes in assessing, coaching, and developing global leaders. He is one of the world's leading experts on global leadership and global human resource development. As a former CEO and U.S. ambassador, and as an author and lecturer, he has experience leading and motivating people in more than sixty countries. He has been a consultant to Merck, Novartis, BP, Doosan, Royal Bank of Scotland, Lanxess, Mitsubishi, Saudi Aramco, and many other Fortune 100 corporations on globalization and the development of global mind-sets, competencies, and corporate cultures. His book *A Manager's Guide to Globalization* is frequently used in executive development programs to help managers gain a more global perspective in their work. He is currently consulting with companies on the development of leadership pipelines that will ensure the talent necessary for future global competitiveness.

Index